"This book contains sensitive, warm, open experiences focusing on forgiveness in the lives of the author and others who have crossed her path. Colleen Evans proves adept at describing the core of the Christian faith in terms applicable to our everyday lives.

"Mrs. Evans was a movie actress prior to her marriage to the Reverend Louis H. Evans, Jr., pastor of the National Presbyterian Church in Washington, D.C.

"The grace of God is evidenced through the words chosen by the author, and she encourages every person to walk free as a forgiven and forgiving person through a personal relationship with Christ.

"This book causes one to examine his motives, lifestyle and reason for being alive.

"As we travel through life at such a hectic pace in the throes of national and international problems, it is refreshing to read a book that addresses the healing of relationships between men and between man and God."

the Oregon Journal

START LOVING

Start Loving

THE MIRACLE OF
FORGIVING

by Colleen Townsend Evans

A Doubleday   Galilee Book

DOUBLEDAY & COMPANY, INC., GARDEN CITY, NEW YORK

1978

START LOVING was first published by
Doubleday & Company, Inc., in 1976.

This book is dedicated

to you

Biblical quotations in this book are from
the J. B. Phillips version of the Bible
except on pages 51, 60, 117 from the Living
Bible and on page 119 from the Revised
Standard Version.

ISBN: 0-385-13116-x
Library of Congress Catalog Card Number 74-18883

Printed in the United States of America

IN APPRECIATION

With grateful appreciation
to Laura Hobe,
whose editorial assistance
has proved invaluable
to the writer.

GRATEFULLY . . .

Ah, but where and how to begin? So many have helped, and so generously.

First, my thanks to my husband, Louis H. Evans, Jr., and to my father-in-law, Louis H. Evans, Sr., for their helpful ideas, especially in the theology of forgiveness . . . to our friend, the Reverend Herb Meza, the Church of the Pilgrims, Washington, D.C., for his willingness to share his collected illustrations and quotations on the subject of forgiveness . . . to our dear friends Helen and George Johns, La Jolla, California, who snip and clip for me . . . and to all the friends who have shared their experiences of forgiveness.

Colleen Townsend Evans
Washington, D.C.
March 1976

CONTENTS

CONTENTS

IV WALKING FREE

I

EVERYONE NEEDS
FORGIVING

Dear Father,

May those who do not yet know the miracle of your forgiveness find it—perhaps through these pages—and let it work in their lives. . . .

May those who have already known the lifting of the burden pass on that gift to others. Amen.

℘ There he was at my front door, the man I had been watching on television a few weeks before. Young, handsome, intelligent . . . a beautiful human being . . . and in so much trouble. He had admitted, before a Senate Investigating Committee and under the glare of television lights, that he had lied under oath during an earlier investigation. He had helped to cover up a crime. His name was Jeb Stuart Magruder.

"Is your husband home?" he asked.

"No," I said. "He'll be here in about an hour."

"Okay," he said. "Would you ask him to give me a call? I'd like to talk to him when he's got a moment." It was a familiar message for my minister-husband.

He smiled and started to leave. I couldn't help myself . . . feeling terribly foolish, I blurted out, "I know you! That is, I feel as if I do. . . . I saw you on TV!"

He stopped and looked back.

I had to tell him. "What you said was wonderful!" My eyes were filling with tears as I remembered the choked-up feeling I had had as I watched him. When one of the questioners asked him if he had lied out of misguided loyalty or ambition, he said, "No, what I did was wrong. Now I want to tell the truth." I could see him sit up straighter . . . and in his eyes there was an expression of peace.

"You know the old saying?" he said to me there at our door, " 'Confession is good for the soul'? Well, it is." Then he left.

During the next few months, as we came to know and love Jeb, his wife Gail, and their four wonderful children, we realized that Jeb had done much more than confess his sins. He had been forgiven—by God, by his family, and by himself . . . and this forgiveness eventually freed him to rebuild his life after he paid the debt society required of him.

"I almost envy him his freedom," someone said wistfully. "Maybe everyone could use a little forgiveness." A strange comment, considering that it was spoken while Jeb was in prison serving his sentence. Yet I knew what the speaker meant by it. She, too, had seen the expression in his eyes and wished it could be in hers . . . she was not free, although she didn't know why she felt bound. She was like so many of us who think we haven't done anything wrong, yet we just don't feel right. As the famous psychiatrist Karl Menninger puts it: "We are made vaguely uneasy by this consciousness, this persistent sense of guilt, and we try to relieve it in various ways." We suffer from a nameless ailment that keeps us from getting close to God and to each other—an ailment that keeps us from loving fully and freely.

Nameless? . . . Perhaps not . . .

" . . . everyone has sinned; everyone falls short of the

beauty of God's plan" (Romans 3:23, Phillips) comes to my mind. *Everyone?* Is that possible? If someone has sinned, wouldn't he or she be aware of it? *Painfully* aware?

"If we refuse to admit that we are sinners, then we live in a world of illusion and truth becomes a stranger to us" (I John 1:8, Phillips). Now that comes pretty close to where I live!

I remember how I felt when I first became a Christian. I was almost overcome with my awareness of God's love . . . it made me feel special, because, with all my human faults, I knew I was accepted, cherished. And faults I did have—I knew that. Still, they weren't the obvious variety. I didn't steal or hate or deliberately lie . . . and I had tried (in vain, of course) never to hurt anyone. So while there were imperfections in my life, I felt quite confident that I wasn't what most people would call "a sinner."

When I asked Jesus Christ to come into my life, I wanted him to change me . . . I wanted to become the kind of a person he could use to reach other people, because, as far as I could understand, that is why we are here on this earth. I wanted—more than anything else—to help in the building of Christ's kingdom. But first I had to be made over—just a little bit, I thought.

"Lord, search me, and let me know if there is any sin in me," I prayed, not really expecting to receive a bad report. Then, to my dismay, I found myself becoming conscious of things I would have preferred to forget. . . . Perhaps I had not exactly *done* something wrong, but neither had I always done what was right. Even when my actions appeared to be blameless . . . not so my motivations. At least, not always. I had been proud of being a "good" person. . . . I had been silent in the presence of injustice. . . . I had worked out my differences with someone who had hurt me, yet I wouldn't let her get close enough to hurt me again. . . . Sometimes, when I had been thoughtful and kind, it was not always out of love for a person but because I wanted that person to love me. I had forced myself to be patient with an opposite point of view, when deep down inside I was furious.

Even more disturbing was my awareness of my uneven relationship with God. Somewhere I had read that sin, in the biblical sense, has three characteristics: We rebel against God and refuse to accept his love, we turn our back on God and live in isolation, and we don't live up to the potential God has created in each of us. I had been guilty of all three.

Yes, as much as I found myself warmed by the new love I felt coming into my life, there had been times when I refused to acknowledge it. I still had moments of self-doubt. I still thought there were things about me that no one—not even God—could possibly love . . . and in that sense I was rebelling against God. At that moment I was telling him, "No, you may *not* love me, at least not right now." And when we do not love ourselves we are, in a sense, telling God that he is wrong to love us. How rebellious can we be!

Even though I prayed for God's guidance in my life, I still thought there were a few things I could handle by myself. So, every now and then, I went my own way . . . a very lonely road indeed.

As far as my potential was concerned, I was far from letting God work freely in my life. . . . I was not allowing him to stretch me and shape me. I just didn't realize that I—

along with all God's children—had a potential waiting to be reached.

Yes, I had sinned, and the knowledge of it made me uncomfortable. Because of something I had done—or not done—I had become separated, cut off, from God and from other men and women . . . and that is what sin is all about. I had asked Christ into my life, but I was not letting him express himself through me. I was still trying to live up to *my* standards of behavior, not his, and there is a vast difference between the two.

Once I began to think about the word *sin*, I realized that it is not restricted to crimes of murder or thievery or treachery, such as we might find in Shakespeare's tragedies. It is far more common. It is, in fact, a universal human condition.

Everyone, at times, has refused to be loved, accepted, and enjoyed by God. Everyone has insisted on doing things his way instead of God's way . . . and who has not fallen short of the mark God sets for each of us? Everyone has moments when he or she has been selfish, apathetic, cynical, greedy, dishonest, defensive, ambitious, joyless. We say we have our reasons, that it's an unpleasant world. Many of us are concerned with the wrongs we see in our lives, in our society, our government, our nation, and our world. Every day we seem to find more reasons to become angry, to hate and want to hit back at the hurt we feel has been done to us. And so we feel more alienated, more lonely than ever before. We know that God wants us to behave in other ways, yet we think he just doesn't understand how tough life is for us, and so we make up our own standards by which to live.

But now we are finding that we can't put things back together again with our hate. Only love can rebuild, and we don't know how to love any more. Something keeps getting in the way of it. . . . When someone hurts us, or when we hurt another person, we often say that "Something has come between us." This is where we are today—with so much between us and our fellow man and God. As I read somewhere —and cannot find the source again—"He that cannot forgive others breaks the bridge over which he himself must pass if he would ever reach heaven; for everyone has need to be forgiven."

A nameless ailment? No . . . it has a name and the word is *sin*. But fortunately, we have a Doctor and there is an antidote. If we will allow our Lord to teach us the meaning of forgiveness . . . and if we will make his forgiveness a part of our moment-to-moment existence . . . then we will be able to love again. The distance between ourselves and God and others will be closed, and we ourselves will be healed of the guilt, anxiety, and loneliness that plague us.

But first—we have to deal with that vague, uneasy sense of guilt . . . we have to be honest with the Doctor about the nature of our ailment. We have to examine the wrongs we have done, the right things we haven't done, and the unpleasant motivations that indicate we are not as OK as we think we are.

CHAPTER 1

"I Did Something Wrong!"

ᕤ There are days when I don't like to open my newspaper. Everything I read is shocking, depressing, painful, or sad. . . . The world is *not* like that—at least, not all of it. Can it be that some newspaper editors believe they can sell more copies by emphasizing all the bad things that happen? Is this just a maneuver to get a reader's attention?

Deliberate sin is difficult for me to understand . . . it means that someone purposefully sets out to hurt someone else, and I don't want to accept that as fact. Deliberate sin is in the minority, I tell myself. . . . Of course there is pain in this world—and I don't want to hide from it—I need to be aware. But there is another side. . . .

And then I open my front door to get my newspaper and see the headlines lying there at my feet—someone has left a bomb in a locker in a busy airline terminal . . . it's the holiday season and so many people are traveling to be with friends and relatives . . . and the bomb goes off and kills and maims. Why? . . . Would it make any difference if we knew why? The fact is, someone intended to hurt and destroy other persons. Someone knew that what he was doing was wrong, yet he went ahead and did it. The enormity of the crime offsets the fact that it isn't the kind of thing that happens every day.

But am I right in making that assumption? We don't read about bombs going off every day, yet there are many other ways in which lives are destroyed—deliberately. When a person does something wrong—and knows it—he is putting his own law before the law of God and the law of other human beings. His needs come first—never mind anyone else's—and that can be very destructive.

Adam and Eve were like that. They were aware of what they were doing when they sinned, but in their minds their need for power was more important to them than the need to be obedient to God.

Well, now . . . that brings deliberate sin down to a level I can understand. I always think of Adam and Eve as ordinary human beings—not monsters of depravity, not terrorists. People like them are hardly in the minority, are they?

The realization makes me uneasy. If Adam and Eve were ordinary human beings—like me and like just about every other person I have ever known—then that must mean everyone is capable of deliberate sin. And conversely, it must mean that people who leave bombs in airport lockers are capable of behaving decently in some other areas of their lives. The acts of deliberate sin may be in the minority, but the sinners definitely are not! We are everywhere.

Some years ago, in a church we were serving, a very sad-eyed beautiful young woman began coming to service every Sunday. Because she was obviously lonely, many people stopped to say a few words to her as she made her way out of the sanctuary each week. She was grateful for their friendliness, almost hungry for their acquaintance. When a young couple invited her to stay for coffee one Sunday, she accepted shyly, and then eagerly. She lived alone, she told them, and hadn't made any friends since coming to the city. It didn't take her long to make friends at the church. She was a delightful girl—thoughtful, warm, loving, and generous. But still there was that sadness about her . . . it kept others from getting close to her.

One lovely fall evening a group from the church were going for an outing. The girl had been very excited about the event, so when she didn't show up by the time everyone was ready to leave, her friends were concerned. One young woman elected to stay at the church and wait for her while the others went ahead.

About a half hour after the others had left, the girl arrived, her face stained with tears. She was terribly upset. Her friend put her arms around her, trying to calm her, but the girl wanted to talk. "Please, let me tell you what I couldn't tell you before!" the girl pleaded.

And then it all came out. . . . The girl was in love with a married man who worked in her office. She had known he was married when she first was attracted to him but she didn't care. She was lonely and she had never known a close relationship. The man was kind, attentive, and appreciative, and for the first time in her life the girl felt important—loved. She began having dinner with the man, but in time they became lovers. In the very beginning he told her he would never leave his wife and son—but at the same time he wanted her. She accepted that arrangement. She would have agreed to anything in order to hold on to him, because she thought she couldn't go on living without him. She needed him—and that was more important to her than the realization that she was involved in an unhealthy relationship.

I don't know why she finally began to attend church. Perhaps she had an even greater need—for a greater love. But something began to happen to her as she sat in the pew Sunday after Sunday. "I didn't know what to say to God," she told her friend. "I hadn't faced him for a long, long time. So I waited for him to say something to me.

"I expected all kinds of accusations, but there was nothing like that. All I felt was love—a different kind of love than I already had. I felt lifted up instead of pulled down.

"That's when I knew I had to do something about my life."

The girl was uneasy. For the first time she could see past her own desperate loneliness to one of the persons she was hurting—the wife of the man she loved. She didn't even know the woman, and perhaps the woman didn't know about her, but she was hurting her just the same and she knew she had to stop. How? She didn't know. She loved the man as much as ever, and he wouldn't let her go without a struggle. She wasn't strong enough to break off the relationship.

The next Sunday was the day a couple invited her to have coffee after church . . . and there were laughter and conversation, genuine interest and warm handclasps. When she went home she knew that something had come into her life that day—and with it was a message from God: She didn't have to be strong—Christ had all the strength she needed—

she would survive the broken relationship because something would replace the emptiness in her life.

That night she ended it. She told the man how she felt and said she did not think she should see him again. She asked for his help and he agreed to stay away from her.

The agreement didn't last long. One night in the middle of the week the man came to her door, begging to talk to her. Overcome with pity and still very much in love with him, she let him in. He wanted her back, he told her. He still didn't want to leave his family but he wanted the girl as well.

The girl gave in and let him stay, but the next morning she knew she had to begin all over again. When the man returned a few nights later, she refused to open her door. That was why she was late arriving for the outing . . . she had waited until he went away.

"I can't go back there," she told her friend. "I don't want to see him yet . . . I need time to get over him."

"You can stay at our house," her friend said. "We have plenty of room, and you can stay for as long as you like."

The girl realized that God was already beginning to end her loneliness. She was about to become part of a wonderful, loving family who accepted her as if she were their own. Too grateful to speak, she threw her arms around her friend and held her tight.

Much time has passed. The girl, with God's support, is still rebuilding her life, and sometimes the process is painful. Her love for the man died a slow death—but she survived. She has changed her job, given up her apartment, and still lives with her friend's family. She is working at making friends and becoming involved in their lives. And, best of all, she has become involved in a whole new style of life with Christ. In accepting his forgiveness and strength, the "old things have passed away, and, behold, all things are becoming new!"

It is so important for us to be able to see beyond the person's wrongdoing to the person himself—which really is a God's-eye view of mankind. And since we are not religious do-it-yourselfers, we need God within us so that we can see others better.

For instance, Judas is a person I usually dismiss quickly from my mind because it is hard for me to come to terms with his betrayal of his friend. I would like to think of him as someone not really human—and yet he was. He was one of twelve men specially chosen by Jesus to share his life, to walk with him, to know his moments of joy and sadness, his delights and disappointments. So there must have been something about him that made Jesus seek him out in this special way. But it is hard for me to accept the possibility that someone so honored could betray such a confidence . . . although probably, if I had known him, I would have liked him, too. . . . And that bothers me, because if I can hate the sin, how can I like the sinner?

Perhaps that is the point Jesus was trying to make when, understanding the inevitable result of Judas' political activism, he forgave him for what he was going to do. . . . We can indeed despise the sin and still love the sinner—if we allow Christ to live in us and love through us.

When it comes to doing something wrong, how many of us can cast the first stone? We may not be terrorists or murderers . . . or adulterers . . . we may be the "little sinners" who justify our wrongdoing with the remark, "Everybody's doing it." "Everybody" is padding his expense account, taking home paper clips from the office, telling white lies, giving false information—just a little bit—on his income tax return. . . . "Everybody" is giving too much time to his career and neglecting his family. . . . "Everybody" wants to keep "those people" out of his neighborhood—and out of his schools. . . . "Everybody" cheats on his exams, exceeds the speed limits, and looks for ways to get around the law. "Everybody" eats too much, consumes too much energy, and pollutes this good earth. It's not our fault—it's "Everybody's."

I don't like to think of myself as someone who could deliberately do wrong . . . and yet I know there is that potential in me because I am human. Like the Quaker who saw a man going to the gallows and said, "There, but for the grace of God, go I," you and I cannot claim credit for the times we do not sin. The occasions are many and the temptations are powerful—much too powerful for us to resist. We need help. . . . As much as we tell ourselves that we could never do such things as we condemn in others, the truth is, we *can.* And we do. Whether our sins are large or small, monstrous or "human," seen or unseen, we commit them. It is our human condition—and on our own we aren't strong enough to do otherwise.

But Someone Else is . . . Someone Else can help us put another person's need before our own. . . . Someone Else can open our eyes to the fact that "everybody" may be wrong. Someone Else knows that, in spite of the headlines of our lives, we are not what we sometimes seem to be. Someone Else knows that there is a potential for goodness in each of us. He put it there—and with his help we can reach it.

CHAPTER 2

Who, Me? I Didn't Do Anything Wrong!

I was meeting two good friends for lunch. Joan had already arrived at the restaurant and I met Mary Jane at the entrance.

Joan waved to us from the table where she was seated, and I could tell she was eager to talk. "Wait till you hear this," she said as we joined her. Her eyes were bright, indignant.

When she entered the restaurant she told the hostess she was meeting two friends. "Maybe they're already here," she said, looking around the room for Mary Jane and me.

"Oh no," the hostess snapped, "they aren't." She didn't even look around.

"How can you know?" Joan said. "You don't know whom I'm meeting."

"They're not here," the woman insisted.

"I think I'll look around anyway," Joan said firmly. When she saw that we were not there, she asked to be seated at a table for three.

"You see," she told us, "it's still happening."

"It" was something familiar to Joan because she is black . . . and proud of it. The waitress, seeing no other black patrons in the room, assumed that Joan's friends were not there. It never occurred to her that Joan might have white friends. There are laws against discrimination today, but some of us still manage to put people down.

Mary Jane and I were shocked . . . but then "it" happened again, right in front of our noses. The waitress handed us our menus and when she came back to take our orders, she began with me. Then she skipped Joan, who was sitting next to me, and asked Mary Jane what she would like.

Mary Jane was quick to sense what was happening and said, "I believe my friend will order next," and Joan took it from there. She gave the waitress her order, and then Mary Jane ordered.

The waitress didn't scowl, neither did she apologize. I don't think she was even aware of what she had done . . . and that was the worst part of it. As far as she was concerned she hadn't done anything wrong. She had simply done her job.

Usually we think of sin as something we *do* . . . but perhaps we hurt people more often by the things we don't do. It's easier for us to be careful about what we do . . . but, oh, the things we leave undone!

I've heard—and I guess everyone else has—that when a person is close to death, it is not unusual for his whole life to flash before him. In an instant he becomes aware of things he has done all through the years, many of which fill him with remorse.

Now, I am sure that we all are close to death at different times in our lives, without even knowing it. . . . If we had taken that earlier train, the one that derailed . . . If we had been at the airport when that bomb went off . . . But for me, there was a time when I was near death—and I knew it. As I lay in the back seat of the car, speeding through Los Angeles traffic toward Hollywood Presbyterian Hospital, my life did parade through my mind, and in an incredibly short amount of time. But it was not so much the things I had *done* as the things I had *not* done that left their mark on my heart. People I loved, and had not told nearly often enough . . . people I wanted to be with and do special things for, but had been too busy to squeeze into my life . . . And my family—it would be impossible to describe the love and tenderness I felt toward them . . . and the intensity of my desire to be for them all God intended me to be.

I was one grateful woman when—some time later, after emergency surgery and after the miracle of new life and healing filled my body—I was returned to my family. From that moment on I became determined to put people before programs, to give those who are closest to me the priority they deserve. I found a new freedom—the strength to say No to all kinds of requests that were good in themselves but would ultimately keep me from being and doing God's best. It was a freedom I needed.

And so, when I came to this chapter—"Who, me? I didn't do anything wrong!"—a special chord in my heart responded. We hear much about the sins of commission—now, what about the sins of omission? Isn't it sometimes true that the greatest pain we can inflict is not by the things we do, but by the things we leave undone?

The playwright George Bernard Shaw, who seemed to have some knowledge of what sin was all about, wrote, "The worst sin toward our fellow creatures is not to hate them, but to be indifferent to them: That's the essence of inhumanity."

"The essence of inhumanity" . . . what a thought! Not many of us overtly hate our sisters and brothers—we're too nice, too civilized for that. We simply ignore them!

As I think about Jesus' story of the Good Samaritan, I realize that the really bad guys were not the robbers who left their victim wounded by the side of the road, but the admired and respected people who looked the other way as they passed by the wounded man. Their silence—the way they ignored the human need—cried out through the centuries, "I don't care!"

"Remember that if a man knows what is right and fails to do it, his failure is a real sin" (James 4:17, Phillips). Could it be that indifference is the true opposite of love?

Indifference turns people into things, into objects unworthy of response . . . and that can hurt. I know . . . it's happened to me. I remember a time when a woman and I had entirely different points of view on an important issue before a committee on which we both served. I tried to explain my feelings to her after the meeting, but before I could say more than a few words, the woman interrupted.

"Really," she said coolly, "it isn't that important. It doesn't matter to me." Then she walked away.

That hurt! I felt rejected . . . and yet, she didn't *do* anything. That's just the point—she didn't listen to me, she didn't acknowledge my desire to communicate with her, she didn't consider me worth her time. She ignored me.

We can ignore people in so many ways—we don't have to brush them off. We can even give someone plenty of attention—and still ignore their most important needs.

When I was a very young actress under contract to a motion picture studio I frequently used to see another young woman who was to become one of the great stars of all time. She was on her way to the top then and she certainly got a lot of attention from everyone. But what kind of attention? In an environment where beauty was almost commonplace, this girl's physical loveliness stood out . . . she radiated sexuality . . . in short, she was a knockout! So wherever she went there were whistles and remarks, some of them embarrassing—to me, even dehumanizing. One day at lunchtime she and I were walking into the studio commissary, and it was interesting for me to notice the different ways we were treated. For me it was "Hi, Coke, how are you?" and a few questions that indicated people were interested in who I was and what I was doing. I was a person. But for the beautiful girl standing in line behind me it was "Hey, gorgeous!" and the kind of comment that indicated interest in her appearance but not in the person herself. Years later, after several marriages and broken relationships, she took her own life. . . . Stardom had been an unhappy, frustrating experience for her because, for all the attention it brought her, she—or the person she really was—felt ignored. . . . Since then I've wondered—Can a person actually die of neglect?

Neutrality is a form of indifference. As someone has said, "All that is needed for evil to triumph is the silence of good people." We could translate that into "I don't want to get involved," a statement we hear often today.

When a young woman named Kitty Genovese was stabbed to death under the streetlight outside her apartment building in New York, thirty-eight people did not want to get involved. Instead they watched from their windows as the young woman screamed and the killer attacked again and again. Unusual? A rarity? People aren't like that? Well, more recently, a Philadelphia wife and mother was returning from the supermarket one summer evening around eight o'clock and she was attacked by a man in her driveway as she got out of her car. She screamed and struggled. Neighbors saw the man drag her for a full block before he pulled her behind a school building, knocked her to the ground, and raped her. Moments later the woman—her kneecap broken and her clothing torn—limped to the corner where there were several shops and lighted windows. She approached a group of teen-agers and begged them to call the police—and they ignored her! She went into one of the shops and told a salesclerk what had happened. Would someone please call the police? No one did. The woman's purse had been stolen by her attacker and she didn't even have a coin to make a telephone call. Bruised, in severe pain from her broken kneecap, she limped on until finally she saw a policeman and got help.

If a person is doing something wrong, we don't have to join him in order to help him in his wrongdoing. All we have to do is neglect to interfere. . . . After all, haven't we been taught to "mind our own business," "live and let live," "keep our noses clean"? Neutrality is considered a respectable—and respected—position, not only among nations, but among people.

Perhaps so . . . and yet I know that when Christ lives

within us we cannot remain neutral or indifferent because
he is not. If he were, he wouldn't have walked this earth in
the first place, because that required his complete involvement in our lives. But he could not close his eyes or his heart
to us . . . and if we are really his, we will express the same
kind of sensitivity. In the presence of wrongdoing we will
not be neutral. We will be objective, yes, because we have
to be able to survey a situation honestly if we are to be of
any real help. . . . And we will get very much involved . . .
because that is the nature of love.

"As for the well-to-do man who sees his brother in want
but shuts his eyes—and his heart—how could anyone believe
that the love of God lives in him? . . . Let us not love
merely in theory or in words—let us love in sincerity and
practice" (I John 3:17–18, Phillips).

Another form of indifference is neglect. We may love
someone but neglect to tell him, and that, to me, is a sin of
omission—a very common one. You can find it in the best—
and most loving—of families.

Most of us have been found wanting in this area. I remember one day several years ago when I attended a lecture by a speaker who asked an intriguing question: "Did
you ever tell someone you love that he or she gives you joy?"
I had to think about that. I wasn't sure I had—not in so
many words, and the words, in this case, were what mat-
tered. My husband and my children have always given me
great joy, but I couldn't be sure that they knew it—because I
hadn't told them. I told them I loved them—all the time—
but *joy* . . . I wasn't sure I had ever mentioned that.

When I went home late that afternoon, my husband was
in his study preparing his Sunday sermon. He was deep in

concentration, but I simply had to interrupt him, if only for a moment. "Louie," I said, and when I had his attention, I went on, "I just wanted you to know that you give me real joy!" Hearing myself, I thought he might think I was a little silly—but no, he didn't. His face lit up.

"Thank you, Coke," he said. "That's special—it's wonderful to know that."

When our children came home from school, I told each one the same thing, and the delighted expressions on their faces made me choke up a bit. My daughter Andie hugged me and said, "Hey, Mom, that's great—because you bring us joy, too!" And then I knew how it felt to be *told* that I was loved, even though I had hoped it was true all along.

You bring me joy—in so many words—is beautiful!

CHAPTER 3

"I Did the Right Thing!"

An elderly woman was causing quite a commotion on a busy city street. She was walking along with a sandwich board over her shoulders, on each side of which was this message: "Touch me—wrinkles are not contagious!" She didn't say a word, but as people passed her they turned their heads, struck by the words that so clearly described the isolation of the elderly today.

Until recently the elderly were a functioning part of our society. Usually they lived with or near the younger members of their families, helping to bring up children and doing many little thoughtful things no one else seemed to have the time to do. Sometimes they were ill, sometimes they stubbornly resisted new ways, and sometimes they seemed to live in the past, but these problems were considered part—not the whole—of being old.

Now that our society is more affluent, we are able to treat our senior citizens differently. We don't have to take them in when they become too old to maintain their own homes—we can put them in nursing homes. And we don't have to let them work as long as they once did—in fact, we insist on their early retirement. We build "leisure communities" where they can live together without the noise and intrusion of young people, children, dogs, or cats. Now, if this is their choice—well and good. But could it be, in some instances, that we are doing all the right things for the elderly—but with the wrong motivations? Secretly—so secretly that we dare not tell ourselves—we seem to be getting them out of our way. We are giving them our money, but not ourselves. That is what the old woman with the sandwich board was telling us.

Sometimes the nursing home is the only solution—but not always. Sometimes an elderly man or woman may not want to retire. And perhaps our older citizens may prefer the company of those who are younger.

Doing the right things for the wrong reasons is the most subtle of sins, and yet Jesus said that if we intend evil—and cover it up with acceptable behavior—it is nevertheless evil. The intention is what counts.

We have to be careful, especially within our own families, about our intentions. Are we sure they are what they seem to be? . . . We are quite capable of fooling ourselves, of thinking that our words of wisdom and advice mean only that we want to help someone we love. And yet, if we look a bit deeper, we find that sometimes we just want to help that person run his or her life.

We have four children—one son in high school and a daughter and two sons in college. Of course, we're partial, but we think they are great people . . . and because of their honesty with us, my husband and I feel that God has used them to help us see ourselves more objectively. More than any other people in our lives, our children stimulate us to grow and stretch. When we are together, there never seems to be enough time to talk about all the things we want to share with each other. We're amazed—pleased, too—that they genuinely want to know how we feel about the things that are important to them. *But*—there is a fine line between sharing how *we* feel and telling them how we think *they* ought to feel about their concerns, their interests, and their relationships. And whenever we cross that line, our children call us on it—rightly so! Sometimes I'm reminded of a prayer written by a good friend of mine whose little girls have grown into lovely young women by now—"Lord, help me to keep my hands off things that don't belong to me, such as other people's lives!"

I have to watch it with my husband, too. Being a natural-born fixer-upper, in times of crisis I am ready with all kinds of solutions to his problems—most of which he doesn't need. I tell myself I'm only trying to help—and in my way, I am—but the truth is, that kind of help isn't very helpful . . . and I dislike myself when I start giving it.

During the crisis years of the sixties, a reporter asked my husband for an interview, which in itself was no cause for alarm. But the newspaper for which the reporter worked was known for sensationalizing the facts, and in previous years had not been exactly friendly toward churches.

"Are you nervous?" I asked Louie the morning of the interview.

"No—should I be?" he said, smiling just a little.

"Well, what are you going to say?" I asked.

"I won't know that until the reporter asks me some questions."

I didn't want to put words in his mouth, but I "just happened" to have several things on my mind I thought he might like to mention. Before I could stop myself I was table-thumping about the progress the church was making.

Louie finished breakfast without a word.

"Well?" I said.

"Well—what?"

"Do you think you might want to mention some of these?"

"Oh, I think I'll play it by ear," he said, and kissed me good-by before he left for his office.

For the rest of the morning I fretted . . . telling myself it was concern for the way the interview was going. Then I began to realize that what really troubled me was not the outcome of the interview but the way I had treated Louie—and I fretted even more!

I had no peace until I stopped what I was doing and prayed . . . asking God to forgive me for slipping back into my old habit of being Little Mother Fixit. I knew that later I would have to ask the same forgiveness of Louie.

The interview went well. When Louie came home, he said, "What a neat guy! I think he can help me understand some things I need to know about our city. And, you know, he really *wanted* to know about the church and its mission in the city—about our people and their hopes and dreams for the future." Later in the week the article appeared in the newspaper and it was neither sensational nor derogatory. It was honest—even enthusiastic! And all without—or in spite of—my help!

It's hard, I know, for any of us to be objective about our intentions. So often we tell ourselves we mean one thing when really we mean something else. . . . The men and women involved in Watergate told themselves they wanted their man to win. . . . The person who doesn't want his neighborhood integrated tells himself he only wants the best for his children. . . . Those who oppose sending some of our food to hungry nations who are not our political allies tell themselves they are looking out for our national security. All of them feel they are doing the right thing, as they see it.

As they see it . . . perhaps that is where the difficulty lies. Each of us looks at the world in a different way . . . each of us has different needs, strengths, weaknesses, fears, and goals. It's almost impossible for us to agree on what is the right way for us to live. Each of us wants his or her own way, and all too often we are in conflict.

Motivations are tricky things—they don't like to come out into the open, probably because some of them aren't very nice. Let's face it—some of them are sinful! And for that reason we can't always trust them.

Getting to the truth may be uncomfortable. Jesus used to make some people uneasy because he was able to see through to the real reasons behind their behavior. . . . I can just imagine how Mary must have felt when she and Joseph, having lost track of Jesus in Jerusalem, finally found him in the Temple, talking with the teachers of law. I think I know what was going through Mary's mind. . . . She wanted her son to come home where she could take care of him . . . perhaps he hadn't been eating regularly and, like most mothers—I'm no exception—she was concerned about him.

Sometimes, when our children are old enough to go their own way in life, we mothers feel a bit helpless. We can no longer protect them from the hurts and disappointments in life, and so we put undue emphasis on the few simple things we can still do for them—we want them to come home and eat their dinner! Perhaps that's how Mary felt at that moment.

But she also was trying to keep her son too close to her, and Jesus saw that. "No!" he answered her firmly. "Why did you need to search? Didn't you realize I would be here at the Temple, in my Father's house?"

It was harsh, and I feel Mary might have been hurt by the remark, but I'm just as sure she also saw the truth her son had exposed. And for that she must have been grateful—most mothers *do* want their children to grow up and lead their own lives.

Perhaps, though, it's best if we aren't sure we are doing the right thing . . . perhaps we ought to let Jesus decide that for us. Could it be that it is better to make a mistake with a good motive—than to do the right thing for the wrong reason?

CHAPTER 4

When We Can't Forgive

℘ My friend . . . you turned away from me just now. . . . You don't want me to know there is alcohol on your breath . . . and at ten o'clock in the morning. Please don't try to hide. . . . Don't you know I love you—no matter how early you begin drinking? Whatever it is that drives you to drink before you can face the day—*that's* what concerns me, because it is destroying you. Why won't you let me touch you, reach you, love you?

And you, my other friend . . . why did you begin to weep when someone mentioned forgiveness? . . . . You still blame yourself, don't you? Your husband has been dead for six years and still you think you might have done something to save him. Why are you so hard on yourself? You did all you could. . . . You tried to persuade him to slow down after that heart attack, but he wasn't that kind of man. He had to move fast . . . get things done. You couldn't change that part of him. Friend, you didn't cause his death. You are not guilty . . . there is nothing to forgive.

Dear one, you have been hurt, and in the most painful way . . . by one close to you. . . . You loved her so and you thought she loved you . . . but that's all over now. She's gone. She loves someone else, or thinks she does—and you cannot forgive her. You do not even want to remember loving her because love seems so alien to you now . . . a distant memory, something for the very young to imagine. Dear friend, can't you see you are hurting yourself?

And you . . . will you never forgive them? Will you never put your trust in other leaders? You feel betrayed, I know . . . you had faith in their promises, you wanted to work with them toward a better world, and now you find that they didn't mean what they said. Behind their lofty vows they were petty, selfish, deceitful. . . . You resisted facing the truth for as long as you could, but now that you know, you refuse to accept the promises of other men. You cannot trust . . . don't you realize that cynicism is a sin—because it is the death of love?

There are so many others—troubled, guilt-ridden, unable to forgive themselves and others—carrying burdens beyond their ability to bear. When we can't get rid of our guilt or our resentment, we become separated, cut off—from ourselves, from others, and from God. We can't love any more . . . and we can't *feel* loved . . . so we take it out on ourselves. Friendships are strained, often broken, families are torn apart, some people turn to drinking or to drugs or to compulsive sex because they can't stand the loneliness that has come into their lives. Many of them are in hospitals or mental institutions because they—or someone in their lives—can't forgive and start loving again.

The apostles of humanism minimize sin—and leave us

frustrated because the pain is still there inside us and we don't know how to deal with it. As Vincent Taylor, the English Bible scholar, says, "The true friends of man are those who, while rejecting the doctrine of total depravity, see with clear eyes the sin in individuals and communities which is the cause of all our woe."

"This haunting sense of moral evil or sinfulness," Menninger says, ". . . usually has attached to it a need to be punished." Perhaps that is why a psychologist says that "Fear and resentment are at the basis of all neuroses," . . . and a woman who has been repeatedly hospitalized claims that "My body has been drained by inner conflicts of all power to resist disease." Our need for forgiveness leaves its mark on us.

When we can't forgive, strange things happen to us—in punishing ourselves we develop an appetite for failure . . . we become accident-prone . . . we lock ourselves into miserable human relationships. We punish ourselves in *some* way, for we are very resourceful. As a person sows, so shall he reap—but the crop is one of infinite variety. Guilt and feelings of hostility make it impossible for us to enjoy health —or impart it to others.

Some of us harbor a general sort of guilt. . . . Perhaps we didn't instigate the sin, but we helped to carry it out. Yes, of course, we were only following orders. . . . Sound familiar?

I know what many psychiatrists say about guilt—that it is undeserved, an illness of the mind, a figment of our imagination that can be reasoned out of existence. Yet I wonder about that. Some guilt *is* deserved. . . . If we do something wrong, shouldn't we feel convicted of a sin? If not, then we have lost touch with ourselves. No . . . some guilt is necessary, even useful. It can sound the alarm when we have done something wrong. It can lead us to repentance, to an honest facing of ourselves and our behavior.

Guilt is not meant to cripple us. Once we have experienced forgiveness, we are to carry the guilt no longer. Our minds and bodies should then have our permission to regain their health.

Why don't they?

How often we hear someone say, "Oh, I pray all the time —but my prayers just hit the ceiling. God doesn't seem to hear me." But he *does* hear. It is *we* who have broken the connection . . . because we can't forgive—and forgiveness is what keeps our line of holy communication open.

In Gabriel Marcel's play, *A Man of God*, a woman named Edmee is unfaithful to her husband. After months of inner struggle, her husband forgives her, but Edmee is unable to forgive herself. At one point in the play Edmee's brother-in-law describes her life-style, a life-style lived by many of us today—outwardly good, but inwardly burdened by guilt: "Edmee is so austere, so wrapped up in her duties, so absorbed in good work. It gives me the impression of a sleep-walker. I sometimes feel that your wife is going through life half conscious."

Half-conscious people—know anyone like that?

The poet e. e. cummings has another word for it . . . he calls it being "undead." And this is true of us when we allow guilt to rob us of life. We do not have the simplicity, the faith, and the courage to accept God's gift of forgiveness. We are afraid to take the risk of changing the way we live by yielding to his grace.

But why? Why do we not forgive others—and ourselves? Why do some of us hold our grievances so close to us? I think it was novelist John Steinbeck who wrote: "We gather our arms full of guilt as though it were precious stuff. It must be that we want it that way."

Self-destructive as that seems, I think it is true. Our lives can become like overloaded cabooses—too heavy for our motors to pull. And unresolved guilt is the heaviest burden in the world. It slows us down, exhausts us, decreases our abilities to perform our tasks . . . and on we go, dragging behind us our compromises, our wrongs, our neglect of those who need and love us—a lifetime of junk.

These are the things we can unburden—if we choose to be free, if we want to be healthy, if we want to love fully. Whatever keeps us from doing it?

I didn't really have an answer to that question when I came to this point in my thinking. And then I asked my daughter, "Andie, what do you suppose keeps us from forgiving?"

She thought for a moment and then she said one simple word: "Pride."

The more I thought about it, the more profound I discovered her answer to be. Our pride does get in the way of forgiving and being forgiven. It's an old enemy, but nevertheless a vigorous one, and we have done battle with it since Eden.

Of course—when we feel we are *so* right, and someone else is *so* wrong, we somehow feel justified in not forgiving—at least not right away! If someone hurts us, why not make him suffer a little, make him sweat? He deserves it! Yet all the time we are the ones who are suffering the most, be-

cause, in not forgiving, we are not able to love—*anyone.*
Anyone?

Even God . . .

Marilyn could not forgive God for the death of her husband. She and Paul had been married for thirty-eight happy
years. They had been very close, and they had finally
reached that point in their life together where they could
begin to do the things they had always wanted to do. Paul
was retired and they had more time for each other. And
then, without warning, Paul suffered a severe heart attack
and died.

To her friends Marilyn seemed very brave. They never
saw her cry. But deep down inside she was in agony. When
she was alone in the house she and Paul had loved—or
when she walked in the garden he had planted with such
enthusiasm—she wept bitterly. "Why did this happen to
us?" she asked God. "What did we do to deserve this?"

Marilyn was uncomfortable in the company of other married couples. Their happiness was too painful to witness, but
their discord was even worse. The slightest disagreement
between a man and wife in her presence made her want to
cry out, "Don't you know what you're doing! Don't you realize how much you have!"

One night, many months after Paul's death, Marilyn was
awakened from a sound sleep. She heard someone calling
her name. She sat up in bed and there was Paul, standing
beside her. He looked exactly as she had remembered him.

"It was not a ghost or an apparition," Marilyn said, "because Paul took me in his arms, and for a while he just held
me tight—in fact, so tight I could scarcely get my breath.
Then, very gently, he said, 'Please don't cry any more. I'm

very happy where I am, and I'll be waiting for you to join me.'

"It was so typical of him—hugging me so tight. I once told him he didn't know how strong he was and that he might accidentally break one of my ribs. He laughed and said, 'You just don't know how strong my love is for you.'"

Impossible? Marilyn doesn't think so—"Even though I do not understand how such a return is possible, Paul was recognizable in every way, even his voice. I am convinced that he came back to reassure and to comfort me.

"And since that night, instead of tears and regrets, or asking God why this had to happen to us, I now can thank God every day that Paul's passing from this life to a fuller one was not preceded by suffering, infirmity, and disability. I now wonder what I have ever done to deserve such a blessing."

We are just as hard on ourselves when *we* have sinned—or think we have—and there again the reason is pride. How can that be? Pride in hating oneself? Yes . . . there is a negative sort of ego satisfaction in punishing ourselves. . . . "See, I really *am* a bad guy!" Yet, when we say we can't forgive ourselves, we are telling God that our standards of forgiveness are higher than his—because he has already paid the price for our forgiveness, and it is ours for the asking.

I have seen pride destroy a family that once was warm and loving. There was laughter in their home, and such joy in the presence of children. But children grow up and make their own decisions, which can be a time of testing for any family. One child, a daughter, went away to school and, according to her parents, "That was the end of everything!" She had been a quiet, good-natured child, but now she enjoyed the company of boisterous friends who delighted in breaking rules. The girl was expelled from school, and instead of coming home she ran off with a young man her parents had never met. Her parents were hurt—so hurt that they made no effort to get in touch with their daughter. When she sent them letters, they tore them up without opening them. If she telephoned, they hung up the receiver as soon as they heard her voice. They refused to allow their other children to communicate with her.

A few years passed, and one day the parents received a telephone call from a doctor who told them that their daughter was in a hospital. She was dying and begged to see her parents for the last time. Trembling, the father said to the doctor, "You must be mistaken. . . . Our daughter is already dead. She died several years ago."

He hung up the phone. Tears stung his eyes as he told his wife about their daughter's request. His wife agreed that he had done the right thing. "I can't forgive her for what she's done!" she sobbed. "I'm glad it's over."

But it wasn't over . . . and it never will be as long as their pride stands in the way of their forgiveness. It is a sorrowful home they live in these days. No one laughs any more. The children are suspect—What are they doing? Where are they going? With whom? The parents can't enjoy a conversation with each other because they dare not let their eyes meet for fear they may read an accusation in them. And if they should, what then? Will they be able to bear the terrible guilt of what they have done—and cannot undo, because their daughter is dead?

No matter how misunderstood we are—or how mistreated we have been—we are never justified in withholding our forgiveness. Perhaps forgiveness is a road we are reluctant to travel, but we do not have to go alone. Wherever we walk in love, we go with God. All we have to do is take that first step, which begins with a prayer for the person who has wrongfully used us. And oh, what a weight will be lifted from our hearts.

Forgiveness is a gift, but it cannot be given until it is received . . . and we receive it only by faith. Simple? Yes! But hard!

Is there no other way? Let's take a look at the alternatives. . . .

We can repay in kind—the old "eye for an eye." No—revenge only assures the wrongdoer that he was right to hurt us and that maybe he should do a better job of it next time.

We can allow our resentment to build up . . . until it becomes so volatile that we explode—a slow form of suicide.

What about peaceful coexistence? Can't we just ignore the person? . . . have nothing more to do with him? But in order to do that we have to become insensitive to him . . . and that means we destroy part of ourselves.

Only if we have no need for forgiveness ourselves can we dare to withhold forgiveness from another. That's a risk too great to take.

"I never forgive," said General James Oglethorpe.

"Then, I hope, sir," replied John Wesley, "that you never sin."

Forgiveness and being forgiven—it's a two-way street down which we must walk. There is no other way to close the gap between ourselves and our fellow human beings. "If you forgive other people their failures, your Heavenly Fa-

ther will also forgive you. But if you will not forgive. . . ,
neither will your Heavenly Father forgive you your failures"
(Matthew 6:14–15, Phillips).

A family very different from the one I have just described
chose to learn and live forgiveness during their time of testing. Theirs, too, was a happy home while the children were
growing up . . . but then the difficulties began. There were
arguments, disagreements about the way life should be
lived. . . . Finally one son ran off to Mexico and a daughter
went to live with a man by whom she became pregnant and
had an abortion. Still the parents did not let go. There were
letters from the boy in Mexico, and they were answered
with warmth and tenderness. There were visits with the
daughter, and sometimes she came home for a while.

"The most important thing to us was our feeling that no
matter what our children did, we would always love them,"
the mother said. "And to us that meant hanging on in faith
and hope and support—never letting go. To us, that is love."

When the daughter and her young man broke up their relationship, the parents helped the girl get a fresh start in her
life. They arranged for her to spend a few months with a rel-
ative who lived in another part of the country, one who
knew nothing about the girl's unhappy experiences. There
she was able to get a job and adjust to a new environment—
it gave her some confidence in her abilities. When she finally
returned home, she was welcomed with perhaps some ap-
prehension, but also with the willingness to understand. . . . Soon the son returned—still somewhat bellig-
erent, but more aware now of the love that refused to turn
its back on him.

This family has many problems to work out, but the parents have been sustained by Christ and the ability he gives them to forgive and keep on loving. As they saw it, they were passing on to their children the forgiveness and love God had given to them.

"The hurt, the distortions, the fear—all were there," said the mother. "I think I know too well what they look like. They nipped at me from all sides. But always there was Christ's promise: 'No matter what, I love you.' That became the banner we carried for our children. It reminded us that the *what* can never become more important than the *who*— and they are such beautiful *who's*."

It is not easy to be forgiven, or forgiving. Once we accept God's love for us we are challenged to let him reshape our lives. We have to face our sins and allow him to take them from us, and once that happens we can never be the same again—because as we discover our real selves beneath all those layers of guilt, we will begin to change and move out in new directions.

In a novel that was popular a few years ago, one of the characters made a statement that became quite famous: "Love means you never have to say you're sorry." Well, I'm afraid I have to disagree. For me, love means you *do* say you're sorry. . . . You don't hit the bottle, pull the trigger, become unbearable with those close to you, or bore people with your cynicism. You face what you have done and you repent . . . and then you allow God to love you back to health. You realize, as Sören Kierkegaard expressed it, that "I must repent myself back into the family, into the clan, into the race, back to God."

Love also means that when someone else is sorry, we accept his repentance and heal the breach with our continued love. "Let there be no more resentment, no more anger or temper. . . . Be kind to one another; be understanding. Be as ready to forgive others as God for Christ's sake has forgiven you" (Ephesians 4:31–32, Phillips).

A young woman—a friend of mine—who recently found a new relationship with Jesus Christ, shared with me her struggle to attain a forgiving love for those who had hurt her—and those close to her:

"Ruth Graham (Mrs. Billy) once told me that new Christians are like babies: Their new life in Christ is just beginning. Those words have great meaning to me, for, as one who has attempted to live the Christian life for just two years now, I have often felt vulnerable and discouraged in my faith and in need of an all-encompassing love, just as infants need care and love. What has sustained me in my faith is the overwhelming conviction I have whenever I read in the Bible that I am a "child of God"; and that God loves me unconditionally. I think often of the words in Colossians 3:13 (Living Bible):

"'Be gentle and ready to forgive; never hold grudges. Remember, the Lord forgave you, so you must forgive others.'

"Although only 26, two years ago I felt mentally middle-aged. I found that holding grudges and allowing bitterness to fester mutilated my spirit. With my new faith in Christ, however, I feel a sense of relief in shedding the attitude of criticism and constant judging of others.

"In John one reads 'God is love.' In my own life I have found these words to be true, and cherish the beautiful message, 'Most of all let love guide your life.'"

The young woman is Julie Nixon Eisenhower.

Make no mistake about it, forgiveness can be very

difficult. And yet we know that Christ wants us to forgive—
so it must be for our own good. It must be that he loves us
so much that he doesn't want us to be crippled by our har-
bored hurts—he wants to save us from the ills that plague us
when we cannot love, from the guilt that entraps and entan-
gles us when we will not admit we were wrong.

God wants us to walk free—liberated from our "guilted
cage," as Lloyd Ogilvie calls it, no longer driven to please
everybody—not even God—because we will know that we
are already pleasing and do not have to earn our way to
love, liberated from our hostilities and defensiveness, able to
concentrate on loving and serving out of the joyous, healthy
overflow of our fulfilled lives.

II
WHERE DOES GOD COME IN?

℘ A few minutes ago I hung up the phone after having a wonderful, warm visit with my friend Pat, three thousand miles away in California. She gave me a gift today—a bit of herself—her humor, her interest, her love. We shared a few laughs, a tear or two, our concerns . . . and then a prayer.

Now, as I sit here, nourished by our conversation, I realize "What a good friend Pat is! How I love talking to her!" We could have gone on for an hour—and I would have, except that it was her dime, and my conscience began pricking me. I feel so fortunate to have someone like Pat in my life, someone who loves me, someone who has said, with her life as well as her words, "Nothing you can do or say will ever come between us. I am committed to you—you are my friend."

This is the kind of relationship God wants to have with each one of us. He has told us in so many words: "I shall not call you servants any longer, for a servant does not share his master's confidence. No, I call you friends. . . ." (John 15:15, Phillips). He has said he will be nearer to us than our breathing, closer than our hands and feet. He wants us to share every level of our lives with him—our laughter and joys, our heartbreak and hardships. . . . And when we have sinned, he wants us to tell him what we have done. He wants to know all about it—*from us!* No matter what it is, he can take it. "There is only one God, and only one intermediary between God and men, the Man Jesus Christ. He gave himself as a ransom for us all—an act of redemption which happened once, but which stands for all time as a witness to what he is" (I Timothy 2:5–6, Phillips).

When it comes to forgiveness, we can go to the man at the top. . . . He is the One—the only One—who can deal with our sins . . . "For the son of Man has power on earth to forgive sins" (Matthew 9:6, Phillips). "If we confess our sins, he is faithful and just, and will forgive our sins and cleanse us from all unrighteousness" (I John 1:9, RSV). And he will forgive anyone—*anything.*

CHAPTER 5

Let's Get It Straight
What Is God Like?

ᥫ᭡ I was horrified. Lying there in pain in her hospital bed, she looked up at me and said, "I know why this has happened to me—God is punishing me for my sins."

"Oh no!" I said. "God isn't like that!"

Silently she shook her head—her mind was made up. Not that she protested—far from it. She thought she deserved to be punished. . . . This was the way she thought God dealt with sin.

How wrong she was. That was not God destroying her body, making her writhe in agony . . . that was not Christ telling her she was evil . . . that was the Accuser.

I have known him. We all have known him. He is always right there the moment we do something wrong, waiting to rub our noses in it, pointing his long, ugly finger at us, laughing as we squirm. "*You*," he tells us, "*you* did it! *You* committed this sin—and you shall suffer for it." If he has his way, we will suffer for the rest of our lives.

Let's come to an understanding right now—the Accuser is a clever impostor. The worst sin he commits is to insinuate that he speaks for God. He does not. He knows nothing of love. Forgiveness is his enemy, because once it is given and accepted, the Accuser is no more. Poof! He's gone!

The only time the Accuser has any power over us is when we do not—or feel we cannot—accept God's love and forgiveness in our lives. The moment we feel that we have done something so terrible that God will never forgive us, the Accuser makes his appearance. Oh, how he loves to take advantage of our self-doubts! Oh, how he tries to make us do unto others as he has done unto us. Feeling unloved and unforgiven, we become unloving—and unforgiving.

So, if you think you have asked for forgiveness and been denied, if your sins are dragged again and again into your consciousness, don't blame God. Your discomfort doesn't come from him, but from the Accuser.

How can we tell the difference? That's easy. God does not enjoy our discomfort—he does not want us to suffer. When we do—and when we go to him for forgiveness and healing— he soothes us and eases our pain. He knows that sin is excruciating, and that is why he offers us his immediate forgiveness. Not only that—he continues the relationship. He doesn't say, "I forgive you, but I want no more to do with you." He is always there, even when *we* turn away—and when we are reconciled to him, he receives us as a loving Father, not as an accusing judge.

While there is no sin God cannot forgive, his love is not a holy cover-up. Nor is he a pushover. When we feel God's forgiving mercy in our lives, we are not to withhold that same mercy from others. . . . But that doesn't mean we are to wink at evil. Forgiveness does not allow a fool to persist in folly . . . or lies to go unchallenged . . . or prejudice to flourish unopposed. Forgiveness is reality dealing sensibly with reality—love with a rugged face.

Forgiveness is free—to us—but it cost God dearly. So it is not free and easy!

Before Jesus paid the price of forgiveness on the cross, he told a very practical story about indebtedness. He wanted to be sure we understood what forgiveness is all about.

The setting for the story was the house of Simon the Pharisee, where Jesus had been invited for dinner. Simon was the kind of person my children might call "straight." He and his household were extremely proper and, I suspect, more than a little rigid.

While Simon and his guests were eating dinner, something unexpected happened, something that probably embarrassed Simon greatly. In from the streets stepped a prostitute—a woman to whom sin was not an occasional error, but a way of life. As Simon watched in shocked amazement at this intrusion into his orderly home, a remarkable event took place. As the woman stood before Christ—who was as relaxed as Simon was tense in her presence—she broke into tears. Apparently she saw something in Jesus that was so different from other men—a kindness, a love without lust— perhaps no one had ever looked at her as a person. And she was shaken. In a spontaneous gesture of holy affection and generosity, she washed his feet with tears and kisses, and dried them with her hair. Then she anointed them with a precious ointment which she had brought in an alabaster box.

Jesus accepted the act for what it was—a gift of love. But

Simon was incensed. Disgusted, he said to himself, "This proves that Jesus is no prophet, for if God had really sent him, he would know what kind of woman this one is!" (Luke 7:39 ff., Living Bible).

Jesus, knowing Simon's mind, decided to set him—and the record—straight. "Simon," he said, "I have something to say to you."

And then he told this story. . . .

"A man loaned money to two people—$5,000 to one and $500 to the other. But neither of them could pay him back, so he kindly forgave them both, letting them keep the money! Which do you suppose loved him most after that?"

Jesus did not answer his own question, as we so often do. He left it to Simon, who said, "I suppose the one who had owed him the most."

Jesus was not taking the woman's sin lightly. He was affirming her—not because she had sinned, but because she knew she had sinned and she came to the One who could do something about it. That was the kind of attitude to which he could respond.

The woman's sin had been born of a hunger for love—erroneous love, destructive love, to be sure—but when she saw the real thing in the eyes of Jesus, she recognized it . . . she wanted that kind of love in her life.

Her feelings for Jesus ran deep . . . and she did something about them. Simon was rigid . . . interested in Jesus, curious, perhaps, but holding him off at a skeptic's arm's length. So he did nothing.

Jesus went on with his story. "See this woman kneeling here! When I entered your home, you didn't bother to offer me water to wash the dust from my feet, but she has washed them with her tears and wiped them with her hair.

"You refused me the customary kiss of greeting, but she has kissed my feet again and again from the time I first came in.

"You neglected the usual courtesy of olive oil to anoint my head, but she has covered my feet with rare perfume. Therefore her sins—and they are many—are forgiven, for she loved me much; but one who is forgiven little, shows little love."

What kind of a God do we have? A loving God . . . one who is greater than all our sins . . . a truthful God who is patient with our weakness, generous with his strength . . . a God who wants to live in fellowship with us, his people . . . who wants to reconcile us to him no matter what we have done . . . and yet he respects our freedom and will.

This is the God to whom we can go at any time. No one stands in our way—except, perhaps, ourselves.

CHAPTER 6

God Has to Get into the Act

℘ Two middle-aged Dutch women . . . compassionate Christians caught up in a merciless war . . . arrested by the Nazis for hiding Jews in their home . . . sent to a concentration camp which only one of them survived. The story is familiar to many of us who have read *The Hiding Place* or known its author, Corrie Ten Boom. Her name is synonymous with forgiveness.

Humiliation, deprivation, hunger, brutality, nightmarish fear and shock, the slow, agonized death of a younger sister—not many of us are called upon to forgive such inhumanity. And yet Corrie Ten Boom's faith was so strengthened in the midst of suffering that she was able to return to Germany after World War II and tell the German people that God would forgive them their sins.

It was during one of her postwar lecture tours that Corrie Ten Boom was confronted by a man she recognized as one of the guards she had seen at Ravensbrück, the concentration camp where she and her sister were interned for several years. He came to speak to her after she had addressed a group in a church basement in Munich. He was now a Christian. He was thankful for her message to the German people, he said, but he had come to ask for Corrie's personal forgiveness. He offered her his hand.

". . . I stood there," she wrote, "I whose sins had every day to be forgiven—and could not."

During the next few seconds Corrie Ten Boom struggled with something more difficult than she had ever had to face. "For I had to do it—I knew that. The message that God forgives has a prior condition: that we forgive those who have injured us." In her home in Holland, where she had cared for many other victims of Nazi oppression, she saw that "Those who were able to forgive their former enemies were able also to return to the outside world and rebuild their lives, no matter what the physical scars. Those who nursed their bitterness remained invalids. It was as simple and as horrible as that."

And yet she could not give her hand to her former captor —until she asked Jesus for help. "'I can lift my hand. I can do that much,'" she prayed. "'You supply the feeling.'"

Awkwardly, feeling no love in her heart, she lifted her arm and held out her hand. "And as I did, an incredible thing took place. The current started in my shoulder, raced down my arm, sprang into our joined hands. And then this healing warmth seemed to flood my whole being, bringing tears to my eyes.

"'I forgive you, brother!' I cried. 'With all my heart!'"

I don't think I could have done what Corrie Ten Boom did . . . in fact, I *know* I couldn't! But then, neither could Corrie Ten Boom. She makes it quite clear that it was Christ himself who did the forgiving . . . it was his indestructible, unconditional love that vibrated through her, overcoming the very understandable human inability to deal with so much pain.

And the former guard—what about him? Imagine the guilt he carried with him as he walked to the front of the room to meet the woman he had abused so cruelly. How many deaths had he caused, how many lives had he crippled, how many minds had he driven to the point of madness! Would he ever be able to forget? Certainly, forgiveness—of himself or by others—must have seemed impossible.

But then, forgiveness is always impossible for us—for *all* of us, no matter whether the sin and guilt are great or small. We can't handle it ourselves, yet, oh, how we try!

A chaplain at a home for unwed mothers was counseling a young woman who kept saying over and over, "When I have my child, I hope my labor pains will be good and hard!" As if the rhythmic pains of birth could help her deal with her guilt.

Of course, they couldn't—but God can! God has to get into the act or there will be no forgiveness—only punishment.

I have known Mary Ann for a long time, but only recently did she really allow us to become friends. It seemed to me we had always wanted to be close, but around Mary Ann there was an invisible wall that kept people out. She had been married and divorced twice, and although I had never met either of her husbands, I sensed that they, too, had never been allowed to know who she was.

Mary Ann was a very helpful person and we had spent

many hours together working on a favorite community project. She had a delightful sense of humor, but sometimes right in the middle of her laughter, her eyes would suddenly look very sad—it was as if a cloud had passed in front of the sun and a shadow fell on the earth.

When we moved away from California I didn't see Mary Ann for several months. Then she came East for a visit . . . and the moment I met her at the airport I could see that she had changed. She came toward me with such eagerness. She took my hands in both of hers and held them tight. For a moment we both just grinned, and then we threw our arms around each other. Tears began to fill our eyes.

Now, I cry very easily, so there was nothing strange about that. . . . But I had never known Mary Ann to shed a tear—in sadness or in joy. Something had happened in her life!

My husband was away on a short speaking trip, so that evening Mary Ann and I sat up much too late, but for, oh, what a wonderful purpose! We shared, we laughed, we prayed. We thanked God for Mary Ann's discovery of herself. . . . It had happened a few weeks before she came to visit. . . .

Mary Ann had met a man named Hal, whom she admired very much. Hal also was attracted to her, so they began to see quite a lot of each other. He was a widower, with two grown children. She had had no children from either of her marriages. Sometimes, when they went out to dinner, they arranged to meet with the man's children, which was very pleasant for Mary Ann, who liked young people.

One night on their way home from the theater, Hal told Mary Ann that he would like to be married again. What did she think of the idea? Mary Ann felt herself grow cold, almost shivering. She tried to change the subject, but Hal finally came right out and asked her to marry him. Mary Ann said she would think about it.

She was awake all that night, trying to understand why she was so frightened. Hal had given her no reason to be afraid. He was a gentle, considerate, loving person. Mary Ann did not want to hurt him, yet she also did not want to see him again.

Puzzled, angry, not knowing where to turn, Mary Ann began to pray. She asked God to help her find the reason for her fear—not only of Hal, but of almost everyone she knew. "Why can't I get close to anyone?" she asked.

Toward morning, she was still praying. As she knelt, exhausted, by her bed, she saw the first streaks of light in the sky, and suddenly that same glow seemed to penetrate her whole being. The dark corners of her memory were gradually exposed and she began to recall something she had hidden from her consciousness many years ago.

When Mary Ann was fifteen years old—a slight, trusting, soft-spoken girl—a terrible thing had happened to her. As a joke—if anyone could call it that—a group of older boys tricked her into a storage room in the school basement, and there they raped her. Before they let her go they told her that if she ever told anyone about what happened, they would hurt her even more.

Mary Ann made her way home—stunned, sickened, and very ashamed. She could not tell her family—or anyone— about the attack. She was too embarrassed and frightened. She believed the boys would make good their threat. So, each day, for the rest of that year, she went to school where she saw the boys in the corridors and in some of her classes, and each day her fear and rage and shame deepened. Finally, to spare herself further agony, she "forgot" what happened—but only part of her mind wiped out the memory. The rest—the deep, inner reaches of her mind—remembered by sounding an alarm whenever anyone tried to get close to her. She was terrified of being hurt, of being truly known.

When Mary Ann was able to face what had happened to her, she was filled with hatred for the boys who had raped her. Forgive? No, she knew she could never forgive them! But how could she go on living with her rage? That, too, was a barrier to loving relationships.

"I had to ask God to do it for me," she told me. "And he did—although not right away. It took me a long time to be able to think about each one of those boys and then pray for God to bless him. But when I was able to do it, I really meant it!"

Forgiveness was beautiful for Mary Ann. She looked like a different person—her eyes were no longer shaded with sadness. We talked as we had never talked before—openly, honestly, sharing our deepest, most vulnerable feelings. Mary Ann was no longer afraid of people or of life. She was healed.

I don't know what will happen with Mary Ann and Hal—they are seeing each other again, and Hal still wants Mary Ann to marry him. Perhaps, in time . . .

Above all else, God is love. He also is holy. In his love he has marked out a plan that enables us—the sinners, the alienated, the lonely—to have a real relationship with him who is holy. He has offered us Christ, "who his own self bore our sins in his body on the tree."

What a generous plan! But what a price God had to pay.

We ourselves never could have repaid our debt to God—it was too big. We had refused to live his way, we had turned our back upon his love. Such a debt only God himself could pay. . . . On the cross "God was in Christ personally reconciling the world to himself" (II Corinthians 5:19, Phillips). It was a simple—and magnificent—act in which "God tasted death for every man" (Hebrews 2:9).

It is hard for us to understand exactly what God did in sending Jesus, his son, to live and die for us, but I suspect that as we grow in our understanding, we will be less likely to take our sin lightly, realizing how much forgiveness has cost God. We would certainly be less likely to say—as some did to Paul—"Let us sin that grace may abound."

Yes—when we ask it of him, God forgives us totally. He loves us that much . . . but that doesn't mean sin is irrelevant. God is not a sentimental father who delights in indulging his pampered children. When we turn our backs on his generosity, he, as a holy God of love, cannot overlook our sin. When we don't take his holiness seriously, we run the risk of diminishing the gospel to what Richard Neibuhr, the church historian, describes as "a God without wrath brought men without judgment through the ministry of a Christ without a Cross."

As James Devy put it, "To take the condemnation out of the Cross is to take the nerve out of the Gospel."

Forgiveness—free? Yes! Cheap—never! It is as cheap as God's Son.

I was a little girl during World War II, but I remember those stars in the windows of families whose sons or daughters had died in the fighting. Our friend, the Reverend Herb Meza, expressing it symbolically, says, "God has a star in his

window—a star for a Son who died so that all men might be
free to live in loving relationship with him. I wonder if that
could have been what lit the skies that first Christmas
season?"

I am an incurable clipper. Whenever I read anything that
offers some insight into my relationship with God, I cut it
out or copy it down and file it away. (And I have friends
who share their treasures with me.) Unfortunately, in my
eagerness to store away the information before it gets lost, I
often neglect to write down the source of the article. I was
guilty of such an oversight with a clipping I found in my
files, one which is too penetrating to pass up. I honestly do
not know where this comment comes from, but if I ever find
out I will thank the author personally and everlastingly, for
in this simple description he or she has captured the essence
of Christ's meaning in our lives:

"It had been snowing for twenty-four hours. Knowing
that it had been a hard winter, I filled the bird feeder with
an extra supply of feed that morning. Since the feeder was
sheltered, it held the only food not hidden by the snow. A
short while later a small bird appeared in the yard, obviously weak, hungry, and cold. Searching for food, he pecked
at the snow. How helpless I felt! I wanted to go out and
point to the feeder; but if I had opened the door to throw
out more food, he would have flown away.

"Then I realized that only if I were another bird could I
indicate to him where he could find food. Only if I were another bird could I fly with him, identify myself with his hunger and cold, and let him know that I understood and cared.

"Our God, looking at man, knew that he must become
one of us in order that we might understand his language; in

order that we might know his love; in order that we might know his forgiveness; in order that we might point above our heads to the source of nourishment and eternal life."

James Buswell, Jr., said, "No one ever really forgives another—except he bears the penalty of the other's sin against him." Jesus on the cross is the perfect example of that kind of substitution. God loves us *that much!*

You say you feel unworthy? Join the crowd!

You long, with all your heart, to be a better person? Remember—God accepts you . . . right now . . . exactly as you are. And if you accept him as he is, the miracle will happen. You and he—together—will be able to do something about what you would like to be!

III

THE GIVE-AND-TAKE
OF FORGIVING

One of the great joys in life comes from watching a troubled person turn and go in a new—and better—direction. What causes such a thing to happen? A miracle? Sometimes. Forgiveness? Always!

Tom was a charming child, as most rascals are—but he was rebellious, a prankster, a rule breaker, a flaunter of authority. By the time he entered high school, his reputation had preceded him and he filled most of the teachers with dread. He took a special delight in disrupting classes and driving teachers to the limits of their patience. At home, he also was a problem. There were frequent confrontations between parents and child, each one seeking to prove he was more powerful than the other.

So many complaints were filed against Tom that the high school principal decided he would have to expel him—unless a teacher named Mrs. Warren agreed to take him into her class. Mrs. Warren was an exceptionally capable English teacher, but she also was a loving, endlessly patient woman who seemed to have a way with problem students. Yes, Mrs.

Warren said, she would find a place for him in her eleven
o'clock English Literature class, and also in her home room.
She listened calmly as the principal read from a list of Tom's
misdemeanors—a long list that had the principal shaking his
head as he read. No, Mrs. Warren said, she wouldn't change
her mind. She knew what she was getting into—she had
heard about the boy.

When Tom was transferred to Mrs. Warren's class he
behaved as he always did upon meeting a new teacher. He
slouched in his seat in the last row and glared at her, daring
her—by his attitude—to do something about him. At first
Mrs. Warren ignored him. Then, as the class began to discuss the reading assignment, Tom whispered a joke to the
boy in front of him, making the boy laugh. Mrs. Warren
looked up. Then she closed her book, stood and placed another chair at the desk, next to hers.

"Tom, come up here and sit with me for a while," she said
—not as a reprimand, but as a friend. It was an invitation she
was offering, and her manner was so sweet that Tom
couldn't refuse. He sat next to her as she went on with the
lesson. "Tom is new to our class and hasn't had time to read
the assignment, so if you'll bear with me, I'll read it aloud to
him."

With Tom next to her, sharing her book, Mrs. Warren
began to read from *A Tale of Two Cities*. She was a fine
reader and captured Dickens' sense of drama magnificently.
Tom, for all his determination to be an obstruction, found
himself following the text, losing himself in the unfolding of
a great story, sharing the excitement of it with a woman
who really seemed to care about his interest in the book.
That evening he startled his parents by sitting down—

without any prodding—to do his homework—at least the assignment for Mrs. Warren's class.

That was only the beginning. . . . Tom never missed a day of school after that first day in Mrs. Warren's class. Sometimes he cut other classes but never hers. He sat in the front row, participated in discussions, and seemed to enjoy reading aloud when he was called upon to do so. His appetite for reading suddenly became ravenous, and he asked Mrs. Warren to make up a list of books she thought he might enjoy in his free time. After school he stayed in the classroom when the other students went home and had long talks with Mrs. Warren about the things he had read and the ideas they stimulated.

Tom wasn't exactly an angel in other classes, but the effect of his behavior in Mrs. Warren's class began to rub off a little—for which the other teachers were most grateful.

Tom didn't finish high school. In his junior year, after an angry outburst at home, he defiantly joined the Navy. He didn't even say good-by to Mrs. Warren, who was very sad to see him leave school, because she thought she had failed in her attempt to reach him.

Seven years later, when Mrs. Warren was closing up her desk one afternoon before leaving for home, a young man came to the doorway and stood there, smiling. He was much taller and more muscular now, but Mrs. Warren recognized him within seconds. It was Tom! He rushed to her and hugged her so hard her glasses slid down her nose.

"Where have you been?" she said, adjusting her glasses and looking at him intently. My—he was so clear-eyed, so happy and self-confident!

"In school," he said, laughing.

"But I thought—"

"Sure, you thought I was in the Navy. . . . Well, I was, for a while. I went to school there."

It was a long story he had to tell. Thanks to the Navy he was able to finish high school . . . and then he went on to college courses. When his enlistment was up he got a job and continued his education at night. During that time he met a lovely girl. By the time he graduated he was married and had a son. Then he went on to graduate school, also at night.

"Well, what are you doing with your fine education?" Mrs. Warren asked.

"I'm a teacher—I teach English . . . especially to kids who disrupt other classes."

Tom had never forgotten the feeling of acceptance he had had from that first day in Mrs. Warren's class. More than all the threats, all the arguments and confrontations he had known, her forgiving love got through to him. And now he was passing that love on to other young people. He had learned the give-and-take of forgiveness.

Our son Jamie's buddies made him a banner for Christmas last year. It reads: "Love is a basket with five loaves and two fishes—it's never enough until you start to give it away." Forgiveness can work only if it flows from God to us and on to others. If we hold it to ourselves, refusing to pass it on, we destroy it. Until we ourselves have been forgiven by God, we cannot truly forgive others . . . but once we have accepted his divine pardon, we cannot refuse to give it away to others.

As someone said, "An unforgiving heart is unforgivable."

CHAPTER 7

When You Want to Be Forgiven

♪ One of the hardest things in the world for us to do is forgive ourselves . . . and yet we must get beyond this obstacle if we are to know the peace that comes from complete forgiveness.

Perhaps the first step toward being forgiven is what keeps many of us from forgiving—this business of repentance. H-m-m . . . the very sound of the word conjures up images of fingers shaken in my face, scowls—Wait a moment! That's the Accuser at work again.

Let me try, instead, to deal with the word as God interprets it.

Repentance . . . In the Old Testament, *to repent* means to change one's moral direction. In the New Testament it means "to change one's purpose, or intent—to change one's mind." So repentance involves the way we live and the way we think.

Before we can turn away from sin, we must turn toward God. . . . Before we can honestly repent, we must admit our wrongs and confess them to God. We have to soul-search . . . and it takes courage to confront our inner life. We have to stop dipping our finger tips into the finger bowl and claiming we are clean all over.

In a very honest letter, a mother expresses the misgivings many parents feel somewhere deep inside themselves:

"Our failures—that's the hardest area, especially when they have affected the lives of our loved ones. As our two children step into the adult world, it is a joy to see many beautiful things in their lives. But it hurts to see areas of need and struggle that stem in part from ways we have failed them.

"A friend reminded me recently that even these areas are part of the 'all things' which God will use to make a man and woman who will accomplish his unique purposes. So when thoughts of my failures push their way into my consciousness, I let his total forgiveness dissolve my regrets, and go on to praise him who accepts us all just as we are and lovingly works to make us more than we are.

"He doesn't expect us—or our children—to be finished products now."

Children have to forgive their parents so many things that sometimes it makes one tremble at the thought of being a parent. But we are *not* perfect . . . neither must we and our children expect perfection of each other.

In my own moments of doubt, I have been helped by a prayer spoken by another mother. . . . "Lord Jesus, fill the gap between the love I have given my children and the love they need. Amen" (Ruth Stapleton, *The Gift of Inner Healing*, Word Books).

There simply is no way around confession. We cannot receive all that God has promised as long as we harbor resentment, pride, or ugly thoughts against others.

Confession, therefore, is amazingly practical—it is the act of spelling out our sin so that God can deal with it. Absolution—the release from our wrongdoings—is his work.

When we confess, we do more than admit our faults, we drop our defenses and come to grips with our inner selves, we stop blaming life, our parents, our friends, or the "breaks" for our uneasiness. We take the blame ourselves.

Some people think they can leave sin alone and let "time take care of it." Time may heal sorrow but it doesn't eradicate sin. Neglect will not do, for sin cries out for attention . . . and if we do not allow God to overcome it, it will overcome us.

Some shy away from confession, thinking it is a morbid preoccupation with sin. That's a misunderstanding, because confession is our way of getting rid of sin, not dwelling on it. I really enjoy cleaning my house—not because I take a morbid delight in dirt, but because I *like* a clean house.

Sometimes it helps to confess to another person after one has confessed to God . . . I don't know why this is so, but talking about our sins to an objective listener can help us gain some perspective on what we have done. Of course, it depends upon the person, the listener, and the sin. . . .

Dr. Lee Travis, our dear friend and Dean Emeritus of the Graduate School of Psychology, Fuller Theological Seminary, explains how "the productions of therapy are really confessions. . . .

"The patient speaks in metaphor, parable, innuendo, dreams of the day and of the night, fantasies, and picture language. He tries to say what is not openly said. . . . He wants to reveal, but fears to do so. As the therapist accepts what his patient is able to say and lets him know that he also accepts the deeper significance beneath his statements, the therapist is really forgiving the patient and is helping him forgive himself.

"By forgiving another, we clear the way for him to forgive himself. But first it is well to learn what it is that we and he should forgive. Therapy learns the answer to his question. The therapist withdraws completely as the judge, as a public prosecutor, and becomes a public defender of the patient's right to be whole. The patient must get the past confessed and forgiven. He must travel in the deep paths of his unconscious. He must come to know the long-dead characters in his past in order that he may hold them up to the light of this present day. Undigested feelings lying buried in yesterday's rubble need to be put in proper relation to the patient's current claim of accountability. His own right to judge himself must be valid in including all of himself in the judgment."

How many of us, having received God's pardon, are still unable to pardon ourselves? Perhaps we are all too aware that we—and others like us—fall far short of God's unending mercy. *Yes*, we tell ourselves, *Jesus understands . . . but will other people?* Conscious of our deficiencies, we usually are too hard on ourselves.

When I was an actress, I had an agent, a very dear man and a good friend. After I left my career—for the one I wanted more—Mel and I continued to be friends, and it was always a treat for us to get together with him and his beautiful wife, Rosita. On one occasion, I decided to make it a very special evening because we hadn't seen Mel and Rosita for a long time. I spent the entire day in the kitchen—something I rarely do but truly enjoy—preparing a gourmet meal. Then I set a beautiful table and lit the candles in the candelabra. Louie started a fire in the fireplace. Everything was lovely . . . except that our guests never arrived.

After an hour, we became concerned. Had something happened to Mel and his wife? Did their car break down somewhere? We called their home, and Mel answered the phone. He had completely forgotten about our dinner date!

Poor Mel! He was devastated with embarrassment and regret. In fact, he felt so bad that Louie and I wanted to do something to make him feel better. Sure, we were disappointed, we told him—but it was only a dinner . . . and, after all, Louie and I had so little time to ourselves that we would enjoy the evening anyway. . . . But nothing we could say eased Mel's discomfort. The next day he sent flowers—a huge bouquet of roses—and the day after that we got a letter from him. It was filled with abject apologies and self-blame. That night he called again to tell us how sorry he was—and finally Louie had to interrupt him, saying, "Hey, Mel, stop it! We love you! Now, you didn't hurt anybody, so stop feeling guilty." At last Mel understood. We made another dinner date and had a lovely time together.

The truth is, we cannot even forgive ourselves—by ourselves. We are so ready to blame ourselves that we often feel guilty when we haven't even done anything wrong. . . . We are like the people who automatically feel responsible for anything that goes wrong—someone once called them "blame-blotters." Here, too, our imperfect humanity gets in our way, and so, again, we must go to God.

Self-blame is like an infection that spreads to all parts of our lives, weakening the healthy areas. . . .

I met Denise during a church family retreat. She had worked hard all her life, had helped put her husband through medical school and at the same time took wonderful care of their four children. Understandably she was tired —but more than that, she was being eaten away by feelings of guilt that went far back in her life.

When Denise was a child, she knew that her parents loved her, but she longed to see their love demonstrated, and it never was. Her mother was attentive but never cuddled her children, never kissed them. As Denise grew up, she and her mother clashed often. It wasn't that they disliked each other . . . they just seemed to antagonize each other. After Denise was married, she moved away from the town where she was brought up and seldom saw her mother. But, as before, when they were together, they argued and disagreed over the slightest thing.

As the years went by, Denise began to feel guilty because she had never told her mother how much she loved her. "I just couldn't bring myself to do it—I don't know why," she said. "And yet I loved my mother very much. I knew she wanted me to tell her, but she wouldn't come right out and ask me. She was too stubborn—and so was I."

Denise's husband became a doctor, and as his practice grew, life became easier for them. Still, Denise was tired, easily upset, irritable—her marriage was hurt by her distress. She knew she was taking out her guilt feelings on her husband and her children, and hated herself for doing it, but she could not stop.

At the church family retreat, Denise was able to put her

feelings into words, and that helped a lot. But she needed more than any of her church friends could give her—she needed to get in touch with God. We urged her to pray—not formally, but spontaneously, as if she were talking to her best friend, which she was! We encouraged her to tell God what she had done and admit to him that she couldn't forgive herself. Would he do it for her?

He did more than that. . . . As Denise prayed, she began to look back over her childhood and see things she had overlooked when she was a little girl. Her mother had had a terrible fear that she was going to die at a young age, and because she thought she would be taken away from her children while they were still young, she dared not allow herself to hold them close to her. . . . It was too painful for her. Denise did not believe her mother had done the right thing, yet now she could understand why she behaved as she did. . . . Mother and daughter were still two entirely different personalities—perhaps they would never have a harmonious relationship, but they could acknowledge their love for each other.

One day Denise sat down and began to write a letter to her mother. She wrote for hours, pouring out her love for her mother and asking her forgiveness for never saying, "I love you." The moment she put the letter in the mailbox, she felt better than she had felt in months—years. She wasn't so tired any more . . . new energy seemed to pour into her life.

Two weeks later Denise's mother became very ill and died. But a friend who had been with her wrote Denise and told her how much Denise's letter had meant to her mother. She was too weak to write to Denise, but she read the letter over and over, and when she could no longer hold it up to the light, she asked her friend to read it to her. "Your mother died a happy woman," the friend told Denise.

Denise was able to right the wrong she had done—and just in time. For some of us it may be too late, and for others it may not be wise. One man, having confessed an adulterous relationship to God, felt no peace until he also confessed it to his wife. She was wonderfully able to forgive—in fact, she had resources within her which her husband never knew existed. Their story had a happy ending, but that is not always so. I have known of other instances where the admission of adultery was just too much for one of the partners to accept . . . it was a destructive, rather than a healing, force.

Confession to God is always necessary to a restoration of love, but telling another person that we have wronged him or her is a decision we have to weigh carefully. We have to ask ourselves: Will my confession be constructive in this relationship? Will it heal the hurt? Or will it become a barrier that nothing will be able to remove? So much depends upon the persons involved—their strengths, their faith, their ability to face a painful truth. I would hate to—in fact, I could not—say "This is what everyone should do" about confessing to another person.

Confession may be a release to you, but may place a terrible burden on the other person—perhaps one the person is not able to bear. Such healing—which involves another person's suffering—may not be a healing at all. The decision belongs to God. The guidance of the Holy Spirit is the most practical help I can suggest.

Once we have confessed to God—and perhaps to others— the give-and-take of forgiveness begins to work in our lives. We *should* feel relief . . . peace . . . renewed communication with God and with our fellow men—that is, *if* we are able to accept forgiveness. Some of us can't.

Some of us can't accept forgiveness because we just don't feel worthy of it. For many of us, this conviction that we are unlovable began in early childhood. If we were not beautiful . . . or strong . . . or brilliant . . . perhaps people didn't give us the strokes they reserve for the "beautiful" children. And if we were beautiful, we may have been "different" in some way . . . and with the same devastating results.

If that was so in your life, then your first step toward forgiveness is to believe you are worthy of it . . . not because of anything you have or have not done, but because of God's great mercy. You are worth it to him. God loves you! He created you . . . you are his child, and he desires a relationship with you. That means you are special . . . and somewhere close by you there are people who will know you are special. Find them . . . let God lead you to them . . . and put yourself in the way of a blessing.

CHAPTER 8

When You Want to Forgive

ᴄ✢◠ Children can be cruel—we all know that. I learned it as a little girl, a child of divorced parents who was brought up by a mother and grandfather. How I loved the two wonderful adults in my life! Yet, in my early years, I was painfully aware of not having a father. Sometimes, at school events and social functions, I used to stand near the father of another child, hoping people would think he was *my* father. The worst time for me, though, was the day my little friends formed a circle around me and sang, as they danced to Ring-Around-the-Rosie: "Colleen doesn't have a daddy! Colleen doesn't have a daddy!"

Yes, that hurt . . . but I am older now and I can look back and realize that the children who did it simply didn't understand—sometimes cruel things are done without the intent to hurt, and it helps to know that. Understanding makes a difference in the way we look at life.

It takes two to work through forgiveness—God and us. Actually, it takes God working *in* us . . . and our willingness to work it *out* in life.

Even if we cannot understand why someone offended us . . . even if there are basic differences in the way we think . . . we can still *be* understanding. It's a matter of attitude. We can recognize the other person as someone of worth—he or she is someone God loves, someone for whom Christ died, and therefore a person of value.

Until recently Belinda found it impossible to forgive her father for the terrible shame he had brought to her life. She was very young when it happened, and until that time she had adored her father. They had been very close, and Belinda felt a special responsibility to bring cheer to her father's eyes when he was sad. And he was often sad, for there were many problems in the man's life. . . . One day, in a moment of deep anguish, he forced his daughter into an incestuous relationship, one that continued for the next few years until Belinda was able to leave home. She married, hastily and regrettably. Within a few years she was divorced and living alone, assaulted this time by the memories of her hatred for her father.

Belinda married again. Her husband is a patient, understanding man who has been very supportive to her. Gradually she felt she could trust people—life—again. The only obstacle to her happiness was her poor health . . . often during the night she would wake up with a feeling that she was choking. . . . Sitting up, gasping for air, she thought she was going to die. The attacks came more frequently, more severely, and her doctors could do little or nothing for her. She had a form of asthma for which there seemed to be no physical basis . . . medicines offered no relief.

"I knew what it was," she said, "and I knew I would either die or go insane if I couldn't do something about my hatred for my father. . . . That's what was choking me to death!"

It was painful for Belinda to look back on that early time in her life, but with God's help, she did. "Jesus—*you* forgive my father, and then show me how," she prayed.

Something happened as she began to remember. . . . She saw her father, not as a scorned and hated person, but as a man with burdens he was unable to carry—the death of his mother when he was a very little boy . . . years of neglect as the youngest child in a large family whose members had no time to love him . . . the hope for joy in his own wife and children, and the sudden crushing of that hope with the loss of a job . . . the deprivation of unemployment over a long period of time, and the blow to his self-esteem when his wife became the family breadwinner . . . the degradation and self-contempt that must have been his when he turned, in desperation, to what he felt was the one source of happiness in those lonely days—his daughter . . . and the continued confirmation of his worthlessness by his repeated abuse of her. . . .

None of those memories changed the facts for Belinda. The events in her life were the same as she remembered them—except that she no longer hated the pitiful, despairing man her father had become. She understood him, she forgave him, even though she could not alter what he had done —and that understanding saved her life and her sanity. The terrible nighttime attacks of choking began to subside and finally stopped. . . . Belinda slept peacefully.

We don't have to approve of a person's behavior in order to accept him as a valued human being. Remember, God's love sees past the behavior to the man or woman. And if his love is in us, we will *want* to forgive.

Forgiveness was costly to God, and it will cost us, too, so we must not make light of it. One of the most dehumanizing experiences we can have is to go to someone—after praying and asking for courage, yet still trembling—and ask him for forgiveness, only to have him say, "Forget it—it didn't mean a thing."

If forgiveness is important to a brother or a sister, it should become important to us. If we say it doesn't matter, we may think we are polite—but we are trying to avoid the issue, and that is basically dishonest. Forgiveness faces the issue—it wants to clear the mind of its clutter of grudges.

The best time to forgive is *now* . . . quickly! . . . without hesitation . . . before the wound becomes infected. If years have already gone by, *now* is the time to let love have its way. This is the moment to do something about the grudge you hold.

Do something? How? What? One Sunday before communion, a minister made a suggestion to the congregation: "Think of the person who has hurt you the most," he said. "Forgive that person, and then go home and write or call him. *Do* something!"

A man named Jim said he felt as if his minister had singled him out—because for several years Jim had refused to forgive someone who had once been a close friend. After the communion service Jim went home and thought about his friend for a long time. The friend really had hurt him, had told a lie that damaged Jim's reputation. Later the friend was sorry for what he had done, but forgiveness was out of the question for Jim—until that Sunday morning in church.

"I decided to write to my friend, and I spent all afternoon writing letter after letter. But when I showed each version to my wife, she pointed out that I was writing to tell my friend how wrong he had been. I wasn't any closer to forgiving him."

Jim wrestled with forgiveness for a long time. He couldn't reach that point, yet he couldn't put it from his mind. He knew that his minister was right—he had to *do* something. Finally he realized what his minister was getting at—Jim had to take his grudge to God before he could do anything at all. He had to let God do something *for* him.

Jim prayed for the ability to forgive, and as he did he began to remember all the things he loved about his friend—his support, his sense of humor, his dependability, his concern. He had been a fine friend, except for that one moment of weakness. And then Jim discovered something very important.

"I've always been hard on myself," he said. "My standards of behavior are very high. So I guess I'm pretty hard on others, too. I wouldn't have been able to forgive myself if I had done what my friend did—and, of course, I couldn't forgive him either. I was too doggoned proud! Now I had two things to pray about—forgiving myself for my stubbornness and forgiving my friend."

With God's help, Jim was able to do both. The next time he wrote a letter to his friend, he spoke of love and friendship and forgiveness—and he mailed that letter! A week later he received a letter from his friend. Then there were phone calls and a visit—a reunion of two men in a friendship that promises to be deeper and more committed than ever before. And Jim? Forgiveness has changed Jim's life in other ways. His standards still are high, but they are flexible enough to deal with human failure.

"I think I began to live by my faith in Christ the day I asked God to teach me how to forgive a friend," he said.

Art Nelson, a respected, long-time member of our congregation, traveled many, many miles in order to forgive something that was done to him when he was a little boy. Art was only two years old when his mother died. After his father remarried and had children by his second wife, Art found himself unwanted, rejected, the victim of brutal outbursts of cruelty. For most of his early years he suffered in body and in spirit, but the one thing that kept him going was his feeling of kinship with God. "Sometimes he used to pick me up when I couldn't even walk, I was so hurt," he said. "I know it was God who did it, because no one else would have."

Finally, when Art was fifteen, he had a chance to live with a family who gave him the love he desperately needed. He vowed he would have nothing to do with his parents again. He thought he had forgiven them . . . in fact, he thought he forgave them at the very moment they were hurting him. But he didn't want to see them—not ever.

As the years passed, Art's parents, who lived in Sweden, wrote to him many times, asking him to forgive them for what they had done to him. But as far as he was concerned, he had already forgiven them, and so most of the time their letters went unanswered. They begged him to visit them in Sweden so that they could see him at least once before they died, but Art knew he would never go.

And then, one Christmas Eve, after having taken communion, Art and his wife, Millie, were driving home when Art suddenly began to think about his parents. He felt as if a voice were speaking in his ear, saying, "You have not done enough. You must go to them quickly."

"I felt possessed by guilt," he said. "I was afraid I would be too late."

Art and Millie made plans to go to Sweden immediately. Usually Millie doesn't like to fly, but she, too, felt the urgency of the moment and suggested they go by plane.

The reunion was so beautiful that Art gets tears in his eyes when he describes it. His father, wearing his best suit and a white cravat, and his stepmother, badly crippled by arthritis, met Art and Millie at the airport. The first words his stepmother said were, "Forgive me for what I have done to you" . . . and Art was so overcome with an awareness of God's love flowing through him that he took her in his arms and said, "And *you* forgive *me* for those times when I wasn't a good boy."

It was a lovely visit, and a few weeks later Art and his wife left for home. This time they went by boat. By the time they got home there were letters waiting for them. Two were from Art's half brother in Sweden. One informed Art that his stepmother had died the day he left Sweden. The other letter said that Art's father had died a few days later. "They lived only to see you once more, and they both died in peace," the second letter read.

For Art Nelson, the act of forgiving was complete . . . and just in time!

Now, we all don't have to write letters or cover long distances in order to forgive. But sometimes—many times, for me—it does help to do *something*, to perform some act or gesture that cancels out the hurt as tangibly as if we had marked a big X through it.

I find that communion is a wonderful means of grace . . . somehow, taking the bread and the wine when I have something to forgive seems to settle the matter. And so, if our church isn't serving communion when I am working out a forgiveness, I find a church that is. I go there to worship, perhaps anonymously, but in the presence of brothers and sisters in Christ, appropriating that real means of grace into my life.

When you want to forgive, don't "try harder." That is not what God tells us to do. God himself wants to do something —*has* done something—which we can never do for ourselves.

When you want to forgive, let God do it for you. Just say, "Help me, Jesus"!

In the novel *The Mansion*, Gertrude Atherton tells the story of an unfaithful husband who finally confesses his infidelity to his wife. His wife, her eyes wet with tears, turns to him and says, "I do not see yet how it will be best to do it, but—you and I must work this out together." What an affirmation—a reaffirmation—of a wonderful relationship in which love had the final word!

Within a family, forgiveness is a necessary part of the daily relationship. It opens the way to real, rather than conditional, loving.

It has been said that "because we love them so much, no one can hurt us quite as much as our children," but children also have to forgive their parents. No matter how hard we may try not to, we parents do leave our imprints in the soft clay of our children's lives. . . . We are marred and scarred by each other. The solution is not perfection, but forgiveness. Children, at some point, have to realize that their parents also had parents who shaped them. We all need God to heal and reshape our lives. To function fully as an adult, each of us has the choice of carrying the hurt child for the rest of our lives—or forgiving each other our imperfections.

Forgiveness can bring a family closer together. . . . It has happened in our family many times. And I shall never forget the beauty of one of those experiences, when our oldest son, Danny, was just a little fellow, about six years old. He had always been co-operative, never difficult, until—one day Louie visited Danny's Sunday school class. He came as minister, not as father, and he was shocked to find his son disrupting the class with his antics. The teacher was barely able to control the class, and Louie was barely able to control his temper. He had never seen Danny like that before!

It was a serious little boy and a serious father who faced each other at home later after church. Louie left no doubt in anyone's mind that he was going to apply some "discipline," but first, in fairness, he thought he ought to give Danny a chance to explain what happened.

The two of them marched off to a bedroom where they could be alone. "Okay, son," Louie began, "do you realize that you gave your teacher a very hard time this morning?"

Danny stared at the floor. "Yes," he muttered.

"And do you realize you spoiled the lesson for the other children?"

Another mutter. "Yes."

"Well, do you think that was a good thing for you to do?"

The little head shook from side to side slowly, the eyes still staring at the floor.

"Then why did you do it, son?"

Danny raised his head, his clear blue eyes meeting Louie's. "Daddy, you've been too busy lately," he said.

Louie was stunned. "What?"

"You've broken your promise to keep our family time—you're away too much."

All Louie's anger left him and he knelt down to speak to Danny, eyeball to eyeball. He *had* been very busy—for several weeks. Each week he was supposed to spend one day with the children and me—away from his work—and lately he had been putting us off, promising to make up the time later. He meant those promises, we all knew that, but there never seemed to be any "later."

"Danny," he said, "I'm very sorry I haven't been with you as much as we both wanted. I'll try not to let myself get that busy ever again—I promise you. Will you forgive me, Danny, for being too busy now?"

Danny's eyes were filled with tears. "Sure," he said. "Will you forgive me for what *I* did today?"

"Of course!" Louie said, throwing his arms around Danny. The two of them clung to each other, and then they got down on their knees and prayed together. I'm not sure what else took place, but when they joined the rest of us for lunch they were red-eyed, arm in arm, and definitely launched into a new relationship.

Between a husband and wife, how important it is to forgive. Much as we may love to guard our grudges and hug our hurts, a forgiving life-style means we must give up these dubious pleasures.

Real love in a marriage brings two persons so close that the possibility of joy and pain is ever-present. I can tell in an instant—from just a glance—if I have hurt Louie, or if I have been careless of love. At such a time the two most healing words I can say are, "I'm sorry!"

"I'm sorry" . . . they are more than words. . . . They are hands reaching out across the distance between us and another . . . re-establishing the relationship, and offering the other person the mercy that he or she in turn will pass on to others. Unless we take this final step—unless the relationship is continued and strengthened with the bonds of genuine love, we have not experienced complete forgiveness.

Sometimes, though—we tell ourselves—this is not possible. We may forgive but we can't forget—and the remembering gets in the way of the relationship. A couple who are friends of ours tell me that when they keep going over and over something they think they have forgiven, that's when they can be sure they really *haven't* forgiven.

"Forgive and forget" is easy to say but not always possible to do. . . . In fact, it may not be the best thing for us to do when we have been hurt. We can't forgive someone by trying to forget what he or she has done—and the more we try to forget, the more we are likely to remember. Our memories may be healed in time—forgetting may be a final, eventual step in the process of forgiveness, but if it is, it comes to us through God's grace and not our own efforts, however well intended they may be.

Sometimes I *do* forget after forgiving . . . and sometimes the memory remains—but it no longer hurts, and the absence of pain can make a continued relationship possible.

Clara Barton, the inspiration and organizer of the American Red Cross, made some enemies in the course of her long career. She was outspoken, sometimes impatient in her eagerness for justice and mercy. Sometimes her enemies lashed out at her work and attacked her reputation. When she was asked about one particular critic who had treated her most unjustly, she replied, "I distinctly remember forgetting that."

I came across a prayer written by Ruth Stapleton (*The Gift of Inner Healing*, Word Books) a woman who has a deep understanding of the need for healing our memories. This prayer may not touch you at all where you live—on the other hand, it may have the same profound significance for you that it has had for me:

"My earthly father—I forgive you for not being there when I needed you. . . . I forgive you for the things Mother and I needed which you never provided. . . . I forgive you, and I see that you could not be all those things at that time.

"If I have ever hurt you in any way, please forgive me. In his name. Amen."

CHAPTER 9

Love Doesn't Always Win

ℰℛ At 4 A.M. I was still tossing and turning. . . . I was angry with her for not letting me try to heal our wounded relationship. How was I to deal with such a person?

For some time I had been aware of the need for healing between us. . . . In fact, ever since she had known me she had been against me—I never knew why. I knew I had done *something*—or hadn't done something—but I didn't know what. Everything I did or thought or said seemed to rub her the wrong way. I felt terrible about it. I tried so hard to make her my friend because I truly wanted to be *her* friend. She was a young widow, a dynamic woman. I admired her, respected her, really liked her—but the feeling wasn't mutual. Friends who knew us both alluded to her negative feelings about me . . . and when we were together in a group there were little digs.

And then, at one point in my journey with Christ, I had a deep experience with the Holy Spirit that left me filled with an overwhelming sense of love—especially for this person from whom I felt such rejection. I felt led to go and see her so that I could talk these things out with her. I wanted to tell her, face to face, how much I wanted her friendship . . . and that there was only love in my heart for her. So I called her up and then I drove to her home in a neighboring city where she and her children had moved.

My heart was pounding in my throat as I began to tell her that I was aware of her attitude toward me. I recalled some of the hurtful remarks that had come back to me from others—and the jibes and digs I had heard and had been unable to forget. It felt so good to talk about them, to get them out into the open. That moment was very important to me. . . . I was excited at the prospect of being reconciled.

She heard me out. Then, looking puzzled, she shook her head. "I really don't know what you're talking about," she said. "You and I have never been at odds. I have, in fact, the greatest respect for you and your husband."

The pounding of my heart got louder. I couldn't believe what I was hearing. . . .

"As far as I know," she went on, "there is nothing for us to discuss."

Talk about having egg on your face! I felt sick. My approach had been rejected. . . . Thanks, but no thanks. And yet, I had felt so *led* to go to her. Surely the Holy Spirit knew what he was doing! Or had I misinterpreted him somewhere along the way?

I kept asking myself all those questions—over and over—until the wee hours of the morning. It was then I heard the voice that was not a voice saying, "Whether she accepts your attempt at reconciliation is not your responsibility. . . . Forgive her for *not* forgiving." And with God's help, that is what I did. Only then did I sleep.

When I awoke later that morning I was tired—but free! No longer did I feel compelled to please this woman or go out of my way to prove I was worthy of her friendship. I loved her—she didn't have to feel the same way. Love doesn't always win, but being able to love is what counts.

A woman who was appointed president of a large department store had a similar experience. Irene is an extremely capable administrator, well qualified for such an important position, but she was the first woman to have the job and understandably she was a little nervous during those first few days. The store was in trouble—sales had fallen off and profits were down—Irene had been promoted in the hope that she might bring some new creative approach to the store's methods of merchandising.

Irene already thought she knew why the store was in trouble. Its merchandise had not kept up with the needs and tastes of young working people who make up a large segment of the buying public. Irene wanted to encourage the store's buyers to try new products, so she instituted a weekly series of meetings with all the merchandising personnel. Everyone was encouraged to suggest ways in which the store could take on a new image with the public and thereby excite more interest among its customers.

Most of the buyers were enthusiastic about changing the merchandise, but a few resented the idea. One woman, in particular, who had been with the store for as long as anyone could remember, voiced her objection in no uncertain terms one day after Irene left the meeting. She criticized

Irene personally and said she wished she would stop "wasting everyone's time with these silly pep talks."

When Irene heard about the remark she was furious. She knew she had to do something immediately or her position of authority would be shaken. So she called the woman to her office and told her that, while she had no objection to criticism, such remarks made in her absence, and in public, must stop.

The buyer was terribly upset. "Well, if that's the way I am to be treated here—after so many years—I think I ought to quit!"

Irene tried to reason with the woman but only seemed to increase her distress. What would the woman do without her job? She was experienced and talented, but she was almost sixty-five years old, too near the age of retirement to get a job anywhere else.

For days Irene was troubled by the scene in her office. She knew she had done the right thing. She had not abused her authority. But she didn't want the buyer to resign and she felt personally responsible for her.

One evening on her way home from her office, Irene approached a church and felt the urge to go inside and pray. The door was open and no one was inside. She sat down and let her whole body relax as she gave her anxiety and concern to God. "What shall I do, Lord?" she asked.

The answer was unexpected.

"I was told—quite unmistakably—to forgive the woman and to apologize for causing her anxiety. I had done nothing wrong in speaking to her as I did. I had stood on my rights. But now God was asking me not to stand on them any longer. I had hurt the woman's feelings. She needed my comfort, not my authority."

On the way to the office the next morning Irene passed a flower vendor. Impulsively she bought a bunch of daffodils and took them to the buyer's office, but as she held them out the woman said, "I don't like flowers."

"Then may I say something?" Irene asked. Without waiting for a reply, she went on. "Can't we forget what happened the other day? It was such a trivial matter. I've forgiven you for your remarks and I know it won't happen again. . . . Will you forgive me for upsetting you?"

"Well," said the woman, "it's a good thing you came to apologize, because otherwise I would have quit!" Not a word about forgiveness . . . accepted or given.

But Irene was free. Another buyer said, "I don't think the woman understands what you have done. How on earth *did* you do it?"

Irene smiled and put the daffodils in a vase on her desk. "I didn't," she said. "God did."

Later she wrote to me: "God sometimes asks us to do the illogical thing, to give up our authority, our self-righteous position, to humble ourselves and do his will. The amazing thing is the great joy and peace that come from such an act!"

No, love doesn't always win. . . . Neither does it lose. Christ, by his example, tells us to forgive even those who have not admitted and confessed their wrongdoing . . . even when they are not yet aware that they have hurt or wounded . . . even when they do not know he said, "Father, forgive them, for they know not what they do."

Beyond forgetting and leaving the hurt behind us, we can

do something to heal the wound. Sometimes this works, sometimes it doesn't. . . . Success is not guaranteed. But, remember—even Jesus did not win them all. . . .

Try . . . take the risk . . . in the doing there is freedom!

CHAPTER 10

How Often Should You Forgive?

᷒᷒ "Then Peter approached him with the question, 'Master, how many times can my brother wrong me and I must forgive him? Would seven times be enough?'

"'No,' replied Jesus, 'not seven times, but seventy times seven!'" (Matthew 18:21-22, Phillips).

Forgiveness is not a formula, but an attitude. If there were a limit to the number of times we should forgive—if, for instance 490 times were sufficient—then when a person was offended for the 491st time he could say, "That's it! I've done my part—no more forgiving required!" And all the other 490 times he had forgiven would have meant nothing at all, because he would not have acted in the true spirit of love.

Jesus tells us that seventy times seven is *not* 490. . . . Rather, it is innumerableness, indefiniteness, endlessness. There is no way to measure it. He says it does not matter how many times we are called upon to forgive . . . we must do it every time.

Under the rabbinical law of Jesus' day, forgiveness was required three times and no more. So perhaps Peter thought he was very generous in more than doubling the number of times an offense might be repeated and still be forgiven. And so he asks: "Master, how many times can my brother wrong me and I must forgive him? Would seven times be enough?"

Had the brothers and sisters been trying Peter's patience? Were they mistreating him? Was he getting weary of forgiving and looking for a way out? At any rate, the question was not unnatural. But it was founded on a misconception which Jesus dispelled with his reply. Peter's misconception—and it is ours, as well—is that we have a right to resent injury and hurt, that there is a limit to what we can take. Humanly speaking, this is true, but Jesus makes it clear that for his followers there is a radical new life-style in which the obligation to forgive is unlimited and unconditional.

The world of Jesus' day lived the law of retaliation, which required that the wrongdoers should "get what he gave." Jesus turned that law upside down when he said, "You have heard that it used to be said *'An eye for an eye and a tooth for a tooth,'* but I tell you, don't resist the man who wants to harm you. If a man hits your right cheek, turn the other one to him as well. If a man wants to sue you for your coat, let him have it and your overcoat as well. If anybody forces you to go a mile with him, do more—go two miles with him" (Matthew 5:38–42, Phillips).

For the followers of Christ there shall be no getting even. When evil is done to us, we do not repay in kind. This does not mean we are spineless, nor do we allow others to walk all over us. To do so in the name of love would not be loving —it benefits neither the oppressed nor the oppressor.

As Jesus' people we have access to the unlimited love and forgiveness of God—it is not our own small supply of love we are to use, for that would surely run out quickly. By accepting God's free gift of love, we are obligated to give the same love to others. This is God's condition for forgiveness.

Here, though, we become acutely aware of our humanity. We *do* have limits. We cannot be hurt again and again, and still go on offering the other cheek. We want to do it—but we just can't. We are not door mats! But then, neither was Jesus Christ. . . . There were times when he denounced the sin while loving the sinner—and we are to do the same.

We can love a person who is sick without condoning his sick behavior. We can forgive the person who hurts us without excusing the hurt itself. . . . And here is where we must draw the line.

During the early days of my husband's ministry I was really annoyed by the behavior of a member of the congregation. He was an older man named Howard, who had fond memories of the minister he had known during his childhood and early youth. He idolized the man, who was now deceased, and compared every minister—including my husband—to him. No matter what Louie did or how he did it, Howard always had something to say about the way his friend might have handled the same thing.

Now, I hate feeling defensive—but I felt *so* defensive every time I was around Howard. Of course I also felt guilty about it and kept trying to reach a point of forgiveness. At the same time I was participating in a small group where we were trying to learn how to express our real feelings instead of holding them back until they exploded. Obviously I was on a collision course with some of my feelings because in my attempt to reach forgiveness I was repressing some honest reactions.

Well . . . one night at a meeting which Howard and I attended, Howard again began to criticize Louie and the other ministers on the staff, describing to everyone how he thought his childhood minister would have handled a similar situation. . . . And I could take it no longer. I realized that I was not loving Howard by just sitting there—silently—as he made his attacks on people. In other words, loving Howard was one thing . . . putting up with his negative behavior was another!

"Just a minute, Howard," I said, interrupting him. "There's something I've been wanting to say to you for a long time, and if I let it go any longer it's going to come out in a way neither of us will appreciate."

You could have heard a pin drop in the room—and a lot of people were present. Howard was astonished—and silent.

"I don't think any minister will ever please you," I said, "because he isn't the minister you loved as a child. Now, I'm sure that man was a fine minister in his way, just as I feel Louie and our other ministers are in theirs—but they are not the same. That's something I hope you'll be able to accept."

I felt so good! . . . And at last I could come to the point of forgiving Howard because that didn't mean I had to encourage his supercritical behavior. A few days later, Howard's wife said to me, "I don't know what went on at the meeting the other night, but whatever it was, it gave Howard an awful lot of respect for you."

"It gave me respect for him, too," I said. And it was

true. . . . Howard and I did learn to respect each other. In fact, we became good friends . . . and I couldn't help thinking that perhaps he always wanted people to tell him how they felt about his critical attitude. Anyway, he seemed pleased when someone did. Of course, it might not have had this happy ending. Howard might have been very miffed— but that is a risk we have to take if we are going to "speak the truth in love" to people.

Yes, we *are* called upon to forgive as many times as we are offended—but forgive what? If we say, "Oh, that's all right, go ahead and hurt me again," we are encouraging the person to continue the hurting. If we say, "I love you as a person, as a child of God—but I cannot let you do this to me," then we are distinguishing between the person and the action. We are letting the person know that we will continue our relationship with him, but we do not approve of the things he does. And this is our right. Turning the other cheek means that we are willing to be hurt again—and we do this by continuing the relationship. It does not mean we are willing to allow someone to walk all over us.

I don't hate someone who has a problem—*unless* I'm letting that problem manipulate me. If I am free to denounce the problem and still love the person, then I will have no reason to hate.

I have a friend whose mother is an alcoholic. For years my friend struggled with her feelings toward her mother, who, when she was drinking, was abusive and argumentative. It was impossible for her to talk to her mother without becoming angry, so my friend saw her as little as possible. She kept in touch by telephone and by writing letters.

One Easter Sunday my friend called her mother, and, as

usual, her mother began to quarrel with her. "God, help me deal with this," my friend prayed, and as she spoke the words, a feeling of peace came over her.

"I felt an immense love for my mother—I could distinguish between her and the effects of the drinks on the tormented woman at the other end of the line. Still, she was shouting at me, and I knew that if I continued to try to talk to her, I, too, would begin shouting. So I waited until she paused for a second and then I said, 'Mother, I love you very much, but I can't talk to you when you're this way. You're shouting so loud I can't hold the phone up to my ear. I'm going to hang up now, Mother, and then I'm going to call you back tomorrow when you feel better.'

"I hung up as gently as I could and did not answer the phone when it rang again later. I waited until the next day, and then I called my mother again. She was sober, and we had a decent conversation for the first time in years."

Only when my friend was able to see past the acts to the person committing them was she able to forgive . . . and love . . . and continue in the relationship. Now she knows how to forgive "seventy times seven."

IV
WALKING FREE

℘ Suzanne admits that she was a perfectionist and made life very hard for herself. But she also had to cope with some difficult circumstances.

Her husband's career was associated with politics and he was away from home frequently, often for long periods of time. When they were married, Suzanne accepted the necessity for Kurt's absences, but she was unprepared for the amount of work she would have to do—alone and unassisted —by the time they had three little children. Suzanne was a meticulous housekeeper—the kind who cannot bear to see a speck of dust on a tabletop or in a corner. She also was a conscientious and loving mother. In the early years of their marriage, Kurt's mother lived with them, part of the time as an invalid confined to her bed, and Suzanne was her devoted nurse.

Looking back, Suzanne realizes that part of the problem lay in the way she and Kurt had been brought up. In both their families, the women took care of the home and children and the men took care of business . . . so, no matter how overburdened Suzanne was, it never occurred to her to ask Kurt for help and it never occurred to him to offer it.

Suzanne was a healthy woman, but in time her energy became exhausted and the tasks she used to perform so cheerfully now wore her out. She felt guilty about her fatigue—in her eyes she was a failure as a mother, a wife, and a daughter-in-law. She was ashamed at the way she lost her temper under the slightest provocation, snapping at the children and bickering with Kurt.

As the bickering got worse, Suzanne and Kurt decided to see a marriage counselor recommended by their minister. Suzanne really didn't want to go, but she knew she had to do something about her way of life, so she bit her lip and kept the appointment.

The marriage counselor, who also was a minister, was very kind, very understanding. Suzanne had expected him to point the finger of blame at her, but instead he was sympathetic to her pain. He asked her and Kurt to tell him about some of the things that troubled them the most. As Suzanne began to describe her feelings of guilt about her inability to keep up with her work, something amazing happened to her. She could still hear the marriage counselor asking her questions—and she could hear herself answer—but part of her seemed to be somewhere else. A beautiful clear white light seemed to surround her, and she distinctly heard a voice telling her she was forgiven. . . . She was not to feel guilty any more. . . . She was loved by God and was his child. . . . And she was to give this love to those who had hurt her.

Suzanne was so overcome with relief that she could not say a word. At the end of the meeting she thanked the counselor and returned home with her husband. The next day she called the counselor and told him what had happened. He understood and was very happy for her.

"My life changed completely," Suzanne says. "I didn't suddenly wake up and feel energetic—no, it wasn't that simple. But I began to discover ways to take better care of my health. For instance, one day I was passing by a bookstore when I felt a sudden urge to go inside. When I did, and as I looked at shelf after shelf filled with books of all kinds, one book seemed to shout for my attention. It was a book about nutrition. I bought it and read it. I learned that I could increase my energy with a properly balanced diet—at least it was worth a try."

Suzanne is now an expert on nutrition and she enjoys glowing good health. . . . I wish I could do half the things she does without feeling tired.

Realizing that she was loved just the way she was, Suzanne became a much more relaxed person. She didn't have to be perfect—nor did her house. It was neat and comfortable, and that was enough.

Altering their roles as husband and wife was hard for Kurt and Suzanne. Helping Suzanne in the house did not come naturally to Kurt, and Suzanne often had to remind him to do something for her. She didn't relish that part of their readjustment, but neither did she feel guilty about it. She understood that she was not a failure and she was not doing anything wrong by living in a style that was different from the style of her parents.

Forgiveness went a long way with Suzanne—and so it should with each of us. If we accept the love that God so generously offers us, it can be the beginning of a new—and wonderfully free—way of life.

CHAPTER 11

In Touch with Life

இன When a little boy was asked to describe Jesus, he thought for a moment and then replied, "Jesus was the best picture God ever had taken."

Simple as it may appear, there is a lot of truth in his answer. If we want to see God, we should look at Jesus. . . . And if we want to know what it is to walk free and live up to our full potential, we should also look to Jesus. He was the freest person ever to walk this earth—and that is the way God wants us to live.

Jesus was free to be himself. . . . Although he was under tremendous pressure from his followers to become a different kind of messiah—a political, power-oriented, bread king for a chosen few—he rejected that role. He insisted upon fulfilling his real identity as the humble, serving, suffering Lord of all men and women, everywhere.

And so, when we are forgiven and when Christ lives within us, we throw off our identity handicaps along with our guilt. We reject the roles into which we have squeezed ourselves in our frantic attempts to win approval. We *are* approved—and we know it! We are free to become the persons God created us to be, free to touch and feel real life!

". . . I will give you a new heart—I will give you new and right desires—and put a new spirit within you. I will take out your stony hearts of sin and give you new hearts of love" (Ezekiel 36:26, Living Bible).

When we can love ourselves, we begin to feel worthy of achieving . . . and wonderful things happen. Talents which may have gone undiscovered, unnoticed, suddenly come to our attention once the Holy Spirit is given a free hand in our lives. Our imaginative powers are released from the bondage of our self-contempt—they literally soar! Our reasoning abilities become keener, our whole beings are more alert. We are moving toward our God-created potential.

Jesus was free to love others. . . . Unencumbered with undue concern for the self, Jesus was free to give himself to those around him, to meet them in a heartbeat-to-heartbeat relationship. People felt his interest and his love.

One of the most beautiful things God does for us with his love is to give us an appreciation of other people's right to be free. No longer will we want to manipulate or dominate or oppress or shape, even for the best of intentions. We will realize that we are dealing with others of God's creation who also have the right to be themselves.

Jesus was free to express his emotions. . . . He could love and let people know it. . . . He could allow the tears to fall at the death of a friend. . . . He had the freedom to be angry.

And we, when we are free, will live in reality rather than fantasy. As we feel life we will express our reactions to it—without embarrassment or shame. We will not be afraid to

own our emotions . . . we will not fear conflict. Knowing
that we can trust ourselves to communicate in love, we will
not be afraid of close relationships.

Jesus was free to risk. . . . Secure in the love of his Father . . . and in the knowledge that he was about his Father's business, Jesus was able to take the ultimate risk of
going into the city where he would be crucified.

So, we, too—as his people—will be free to take risks, to
face the dangers of involvement in the real world where the
action is taking place . . . and where we are very much
needed.

Jesus was free to serve. . . . He was free to be vulnerable,
to find common cause with the weak, the poor, and the
oppressed.

If we accept God's love, it will awaken in us a compassion
for all those who struggle against the odds in life. As we become free, we will want to serve—both God and those
around us. . . . And we will do it in gratitude for all God
has given us.

*Jesus was free to live fully—to love God and enjoy him
forever.* . . . Sin and guilt separate us from God. It is Jesus,
the Savior, who brings us back.

The most exciting news in the world is that Christ gives
full and final forgiveness to anyone who is penitent in heart.
He restores us to fellowship with God . . . and this is the
meaning of a full life! This is our original destiny.

Christ not only points the way—he *is* the way. By his example, he shows us that our ultimate freedom is achieved in
loving God and enjoying him forever. This is the life abun-
dant . . . and it begins with forgiveness.

I started writing this book with a prayer, a prayer that

someone carrying a burden of guilt—a burden he or she was never meant to bear—would be moved to put the burden down . . . to let God do his work in that person's life. Perhaps that someone was you. If it was, then I want to close with another prayer especially for you. . . .

May you know fully the release from your burden, the joy of your forgiveness. And from this time on, may you walk free in Christ. For "if the Son makes you free, you will be free indeed" (John 8:32, RSV). Amen.